CUBE
BOOK

SAILING

WHITE STAR PUBLISHERS

EDITED BY

VALERIA MANFERTO DE FABIANIS

text by
SIMONE PEROTTI

graphic design
CLARA ZANOTTI

graphic layout
MARIA CUCCHI

editorial coordination
GIADA FRANCIA

translation
JULIAN COMOY

© 2008 WHITE STAR S.P.A.
VIA CANDIDO SASSONE, 22-24
13100 VERCELLI - ITALY
WWW.WHITESTAR.IT

Mariette, a large schooner launched in 1915.

ISBN 978-88-544-0179-2
REPRINTS:
1 2 3 4 5 6   12 11 10 09 08
Printed in Singapore

CONTENTS

SAILS

1 ● The brigantine *Sagres*, built in Germany in 1937, is a Portuguese training vessel.

2-3 ● Legends do not fade: a catamaran sailing off Bora Bora.

4-5 ● One of the competitors close-hauled in the 2004 Antigua Classic Yacht Regatta.

6-7 ● Guadeloupe, 2002: the trimaran *Fujifilm* plowing through heavy seas.

8-9 ● China Team complete its first America's Cup experience in 2007.

13 ● Mahon, 2006 Panerai Classic Yacht Challenge. *Altair*, a beautiful gaff-rigged schooner launched in 1931.

14-15 ● Sailors lined up for inspection on the deck of the *Vespucci*.

16-17 ● *Ranger*, *Windrose* and *Velsheda* side by side at the start of the Antigua Classic Yacht Regatta.

18-19 ● The spinnaker is readied in the bows of *Alinghi*.

Introduction

As a child I longed for a boat. I would look at them from afar, and they seemed to me to be the last horizon, the border with real life. Beyond that line there certainly lay the world, the future. For me, a man was an expert mariner. I knew virtually nothing of life, I was too young. I was scared of school, I was afraid of distant and unknown lands, I quaked at the word love. Even so, brimming with confidence, I was ready to measure myself up against the world. On the other hand, I didn't even understand the language of sailing. The arcane vocabulary of the mariner left me feeling inadequate and gave me my first fainting fits. How could I possi-

● A man at the masthead as an America's Cup Class yacht makes good speed with a following wind.

Introduction

BLY BECOME A MAN? MY SEAFARING GRANDFATHERS WERE DEAD. WHO WAS THERE TO EXPLAIN THINGS TO ME? IN THE PORT WAREHOUSES WHERE I WAS ALLOWED TO ROAM IN THE SUMMER I WOULD TRY TO OVERHEAR THE OLD SEA-DOGS TALK OF THEIR PISCATORIAL EXPLOITS AND REITERATE THEIR MAXIMS ABOUT THE WIND. THE THINGS THEY SAID WERE RIGHT OVER MY HEAD, THE CHAIN OF WORDS JUST THREATENING ECHOES. WHEN I FIRST HEARD THE EXPRESSION *DEADWORK*, I IMAGINED A LOW ISLAND, ONE DAY THRIVING AND ORDERLY, THEN BLOWN AWAY BY SOME UNHEARD-OF CATACLYSM, AND NOW THE DESTINATION ONLY OF THE CONDEMNED. *GRAPNEL* WAS ANOTHER WORD THAT TERRORIZED ME AND I PICTURED A THIN CHARACTER, WITH

Introduction

A HOOK NOSE, A TREACHEROUS EXPRESSION, A FEW STRAY HAIRS ON HIS BALD PATE, INTENT ON PURSUING HIS SHADY DEALS IN DINGY BARS DOWN NARROW LANES. *SLIP STOPPER* GAVE ME FEWER PROBLEMS: A LACKADAISICAL YOUNG MAN WITH A GAMMY LEG, A PETTY THIEF, WHILE A *BULKHEAD* WAS A SINISTER SWINDLER, WHO WAS READY TO PUT A CURSE ON SOMEONE FOR A PENNY. A *PORT TACK* WAS A SHELTER ALONG THE COAST WHERE ONE COULD HIDE FROM ANOTHER SHIP GIVING CHASE. WORRIED, I WOULD PEER UP AT THE SKY, WHERE FLEW THE *SHROUDS*, WINGED, AGGRESSIVE DIVINITIES, WHICH WOULD SWOOP DOWN IN DROVES. *STANCHIONS* WERE THE OTHER RANKS READY TO GIVE THEIR ALL. *WINCHES* WERE BUXOM WOMEN OF ILL RE-

Introduction

PUTE READY TO DOUSE THE FIRES OF DESIRE. COMING HOME FROM OUR HOLIDAYS ONE SUMMER, I WAS STRUCK WITH ADMIRATION FOR ONE OF MY CHUMS WHO KNEW WHAT A *LUBBER LINE* WAS, A DASTARDLY TRAP SET FOR ADULTS AND THEIR UNMENTIONABLE PURSUITS. I GREW UP. I LEARNED THE NAMES OF THE WINDS. I LEARNED TO POINT OUT THE SIGNS OF A GUST OF WIND ON THE HORIZON. THUS DID I LOSE MY CHILDHOOD. THE EMPTY THREATS THREW OPEN THE GATES OF THE WORLD. SAILING NOW SEEMED TO ME THE LAST OF A MAN'S PROBLEMS.

25 • The *Palinuro* shares the job of being Italy's naval training ship with the *Amerigo Vespucci*.

26-27 • *TIM Progetto Italia*, Giovanni Soldini's trimaran, hurtling along at over thirty knots in the opening stretch of the 2005 Transat Jacques Vabre.

28-29 • The 149.6 ft (46.52 m) *Windrose* sailing off Antigua in April 2003.

30-31 • The crew are giving their utmost, close-hauled in heavy seas.

32-33 • Soldini, once again aboard *TIM Progetto Italia*, a masterpiece of rigidity and lightness.

LADIES of the SEA

A fine picture of the bow of *Velsheda*, one of the yachts competing in 0the 2005 Antigua Classic Yacht Regatta.

Ladies of the Sea
Introduction

Her name was mary, but she wasn't a woman. even so, it seems she was a real beauty, and charles ii fell in love with her, naturally. she was the very first yacht to be built, a boat built solely for pleasure, not as a working vessel. one day, proud as punch, he even took his sister to see her, but the weather was not very kind and his sister was violently seasick. she was called mary, and the king named his cutter after her hoping to please his sister and win her over to the joys of sailing in his beloved new yacht. this was toward the end of the seventeenth century, and the king, who had a con-

• Isle of Wight, 2001 America's Cup Jubilee: the greater the close-ups of the yachts, the more it seems we are witnessing a dance, a spectacle with graceful, harmonious movements.

INTRODUCTION Ladies of the Sea

SIDERABLE NUMBER OF DECKHANDS FOR THE HEAVY WORK AND A LOT OF TIME ON HIS HANDS, MADE A HABIT OF CHOOSING DAYS WITH A GOOD BREEZE TO TACK UP AND DOWN THE ENGLISH CHANNEL. OBSERVING HIS KINGDOM FROM OFFSHORE, FAR FROM THE COURT, HELPED TO RELIEVE HIM FOR A WHILE OF THE BURDEN OF RULING.

THIS WAS THE BIRTH OF PLEASURE CRUISING. SO SEAFARING DID NOT ONLY MEAN TRADING AND FIGHTING, SUFFERING HUNGER AND THIRST, RISKING LIFE AND LIMB. THE SEA WAS NOT JUST THE PLACE OF THE DAMNED. WHAT A WONDERFUL DISCOVERY! BUT THAT MEANT BOATS HAD TO CHANGE TOO! THE SEA, WHICH HAD ALWAYS PRODUCED HEARTACHE, BRED WIDOWS AND FAILED TO ENSURE A SAFE RETURN HOME, HAD BEEN TURNED INTO A STAGE

INTRODUCTION Ladies of the Sea

WHERE WONDERS COULD OCCUR, WHERE BEAUTIFUL VESSELS WOULD SAIL AND BECOME THE SYMBOL OF THE GREATEST HARMONY. FIRST CAME THE DESIGNERS, FOLLOWED SOON AFTER BY THE SAILMAKERS. STERNS HAD TO BE LOWERED, BOWS MORE TAPERED OFF AND HULLS MADE MORE GRACEFUL. IF THEY NO LONGER HAD TO CARRY GOODS BUT GENTLEMEN OF RANK, THE LINES OF THE NEW YACHTS HAD TO BECOME MORE ELEGANT, ORNATE BUT SLENDER, FAST, STILL FASTER, AND VERY COMFORTABLE. THEY RODE LOWER IN THE WATER, THE GUNS DISAPPEARED FROM THE DECKS, AND A LARGE NUMBER OF SAILS, MADE LIGHTER AND LIGHTER, WERE TAKEN ASHORE. THERE WAS NO NEED TO CROSS THE ATLANTIC IN THESE BOATS. THERE WAS NO NEED TO GIVE UP PERFORMANCE IN

Ladies of the Sea
Introduction

THE INTERESTS OF ENSURING THE VESSEL WOULD SURVIVE IN ALL CONDITIONS. THAT'S HOW IT CAME TO BE THAT THE BLUE SEA FILLED WITH WHITE SAILS, AND THE PAINTINGS OF THE PERIOD WITH SPLENDID YACHTS. THE PASSING YEARS HAVE CHANGED TASTES; NEW MATERIALS HAVE IMPROVED BOAT DESIGN AND MADE THEM FASTER, BUT THAT DOES-N'T NECESSARILY MEAN THEY HAVE BECOME MORE BEAU-TIFUL. A WOODEN BLOCK, A MANILA ROPE, A ROPE FENDER STUFFED WITH TARRED OAKUM AND A KELVIN BINNACLE ARE THE ECHOES OF A WORLD WHOSE GLAMOUR IN-CREASES WITH EACH STEP IT RECEDES INTO THE PAST. NO NOSTALGIA HERE: ONLY ADMIRATION FOR WHAT CAN STILL BE SEEN PLYING THE SEAS ON CERTAIN GILDED DAYS.

● 2004 Antigua Classic Yacht Regatta. The Caribbean setting adds to the glamor of these splendid classic yachts.

42 • The lines of the classic yachts have a timeless appeal and evoke admiration in any situation.

42-43 • *Ranger* tackles the 2005 Antigua Classic Yacht Regatta: the strongest suit of classics like this yacht, besides their beauty, is their seaworthiness.

44-45 • Unlike the "Martians" wandering the world and racing in extreme regattas, the hands on classic yachts are always elegant, in keeping with the boats they are handling.

46-47 ● An exciting dogfight at the start of the 2005 Antigua Classic Yacht Regatta.

47 ● Compared with monotype class regattas, races between classic yachts seem to bring out all the differences in rig and other details. Every boat is unique.

48-49 ● In spite of the addition of modern materials (often sneered at by purists), the beauty of the classic yachts still relies heavily on wood.

50-51 ● A number of bows seeking an early advantage in the 2005 Antigua Classic Yacht Regatta.

52-53 ● The gennaker is hauled down on the majestic J-Class *Ranger*, skippered by the great Peter Holmberg during the 2005 Antigua Classic Yacht Regatta.

53 ● Commas, brackets and clouds. The flowing white sails of *Velsheda* describe curious shapes in the sky and on the sea.

Velsheda, a high-performance J-Class yacht, shown here competing in a series of Caribbean races for classic yachts, the 2005 Antigua Classic Week.

56-57 • J-Class
yachts carry very large
crews. In this picture,
taken on *Velsheda*,
some are busier than
others. This is 2004
Classic Yachting, too.

58-59 • A spray hood
is enough to spoil the
lines of this fine classic
yacht competing in the
Antigua Classic Yacht
Regatta in April 2004.
Still, the play of light on
the keel is quite
breathtaking.

60 ● An exciting dogfight between *Ranger*, *Windrose* and *Velsheda* during the 2004 Antigua Classic Week.

60-61 ● A speed test between two J-Class yachts, *Ranger* and *Velsheda*, off Antigua, in April 2004.

62 and 62-63 ● Antigua, 2004. Slim and beautiful, the yawl on the left shows off its wooden masts and teak decks. But some classic yachts have been modified: on the right can be seen metal masts and a deck of an unusual color.

64-65 ● Two yawls in action in the Antigua Classic, in April 2004. The one lying to windward, with no mizzen, appears to be more stable and certainly no slower.

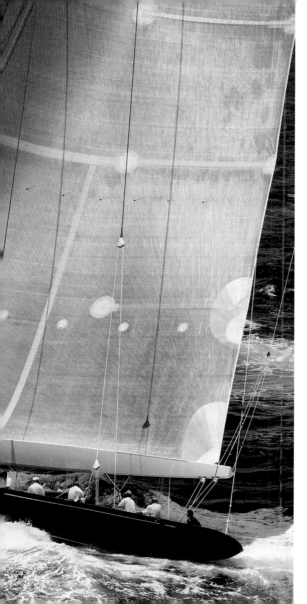

66-67 • *Ranger*, *Windrose* and *Velsheda* racing in Antigua in 2004. One of the glories of these maxi classic yachts is the amount of sail they manage to put on, and the size of their mainsails is especially impressive.

67 • Expert handling under full sail underlines the beauty of these boats, as demonstrated by this yacht racing off Antigua in 2004.

Designed as splendid examples of sea-going yachts, *Ranger* and *Velsheda* (seen here off Antigua, in 2004) are extremely solid and here display all their power and seaworthiness.

70 • Clashes in the seas off Antigua in 2004: the duellists seem to be on the same tack, but actually the J-Class yacht to leeward has veered and is bearing away.

71 • Bowling along past Antigua in 1999, the ketch in the foreground has shortened its mainsail but does not seem to be going any slower.

● *Velsheda* again, off Antigua in 2003. The bow wave sneaks in between the hull and the genoa, putting the sail at risk.

74-75 ● The beautiful lines of
Eleonora's bows slicing through
the waters off Antigua in 2003.

75 ● Hard at work in the bows
of *Windrose*, once again off
Antigua in 2003.

- In spite of having efficient, modern materials, classic yachts (in this case *Windrose*, on the left and *Velsheda*, on the right, off Antigua in April 2003) require an expert crew and a good deal of energy to complete the maneuvers.

The 2007 Antigua Classic Yacht Regatta. Every year the classic regattas attract more and more competitors.

80 • The telling effect of a detail. The J-Class yacht *Ranger* showing off in Antiguan waters, in 2006. This yacht is worth a close look: a real work of art.

81 • *Ashanti IV* shudders under a wave off Antigua, in 2006. A sailor's life is never easy, even on a classic yacht.

82-83 • *Velsheda*'s majestic sails urged on by the wind off Antigua.

The lines of *Avel*, a beautiful gaff-rigged sloop, are set off by Lérins Monastery, on an island off Saint-Tropez. The occasion is the regatta that takes its name from the famous town on the Côte d'Azur.

86-87 • *Astra* and *Candida* in a tight tussle off Saint-Tropez. The two boats have been registered as J-Class yachts since 1933.

88-89 • In some shots the majestic classic yachts seem to be part of the sea itself. Here we see *Moonbeam IV* in action off Saint-Tropez.

Les Voiles de Saint-Tropez, 2004: a fleet of yachts files past the famous church.

92 ● A beautiful shot of *Cambria*, a sloop fully 134.5 ft
(41 m) long, launched in 1928.

93 ● This telephoto picture brings out the energy as well as the beauty of its subject,
Number 1, racing in Les Voiles de Saint-Tropez.

94-95 ● The elegance of the sails of *Thendara*, a 121 ft (37 m) yacht launched in 1937.

● The greatest attraction of classic yacht regattas lies in the uniqueness of each boat (pictured here, Les Voiles de Saint-Tropez; right, a fine shot from the deck of *Mariquita*).

98 • *Tuiga*, with her unmistakeable free board almost at the waterline, during the Saint-Trop regatta.

98-99 • The complex web of ropes wrapped around *Eleonora*'s sails stands out against the stormy sky off Saint-Tropez.

100-101 • The 125 ft (38 m) *Mariquita* is often the boat to beat among the gaff-rigged classic yachts.

101 • The stunning 98 ft (30 m) Wally *Alexia* "gate crashes" Les Voiles de Saint-Tropez.

Different rigs and sails stand out against the sun on a hot afternoon in Saint-Tropez. *Créole* parades her beauty outlined on the right.

● A breath of magic sweeps through the Baie des Canebiers during Les Voiles de Saint-Tropez. Not fewer than 250 boats of all classes congregate here: a unique event in the yachting world.

Velsheda is on her way, with the bowman peering at the horizon in the seas off Saint-Tropez, in 2006.

108 • A spectacular crossing of boats of entirely different size, rig and tack, at Les Voiles de Saint-Tropez, in 2006.

109 • *Eleonora*, without her topmost sails. Saint-Tropez had strong winds in 2006.

A large sails area makes boats very sensitive to weight distribution. All hands have to keep to windward with the boat heeling over – but there are maneuvers to be made. The pictures show the Saint-Tropez races during the 8th Les Voiles, in 2006.

● Saint-Tropez on 3rd October 2006: expert sailors show their acrobatic skills in the bows and at the masthead.

114-115 • Beautiful and piling on the speed, *Moonbeam IV* plunges through the waves at the 2006 Les Voiles at Saint-Tropez.

115 • With light wind conditions everyone is on the leeward side on *Moonbeam IV*.

The technologically advanced Wally boats racing at Saint-Tropez, in 2006. Eight of these titans are competing: *Dangerous But Fun*, *Dark Shadow*, *J One*, *Magic Carpet Squared*, *Nariida*, *Open Season*, *Tango* and *Y3K*.

● The whole sailing fraternity gathers in classic yacht regattas like Les Voiles (shown here in 2006).

Thrills at Saint-Tropez, in October 2006; a memorable meeting, with 280 boats and 3000 crew members.

122 • The winds favor the sails of the gaff-rigged *Bona Fide*, winner of the 2006 Panerai Classic Yachts Challenge. Here she is shown competing at Saint-Tropez, in 2006.

123 • The 2006 Saint-Tropez meeting featured strong winds. The top sails have been hauled down and the gaffs lowered. Less sail area exposed to the wind means greater stability.

The lens zooms in on two thoroughbreds in the 2005 Classic Week. One of these is *Moonbeam III*, launched in 1903.

● The titanic J-Class yachts make a fascinating and atmospheric picture at the 2005 Classic Week. A light wind, and the mainsails are set to catch the lightest breeze.

Moonbeam of Fyfe III (1903) and *Mariette* (1913) at Cannes in 2005. These masterpieces of boatbuilding are by Fife and Herreshoff.

● *Altair* and *Mariette* in a dogfight during the 2005 Régates Royales, at Cannes.

132 • Cannes, 2006. *Mariquita* and *Cambria* in the foreground.

132-133 • The fleet sometimes includes real sailing legends: on the right, one of the great Eric Tabarly's *Pen Duick* boats.

A view of the majestic stern of Lulworth, 151 ft (46 m) of elegance.

● The wind creates almost surreal masterpieces playing with the sailing rigs,
as shown by the three-masted schooner on the left and Mariquita, on the right,
captured during the 2006 Régates Royales.

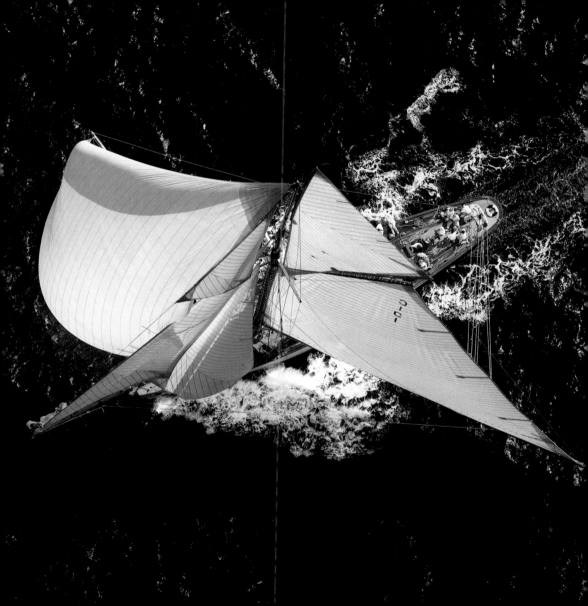

● *Altair*'s billowing
sails completely hide
her hull.

140 • One boat or two? The now famous picture of *Little Jap* and *Mariquita* overlapping one another.

141 • Fife's *Cintra* rounds l'Église de Saint-Tropez.

142-143 • Shadows and reflections as *Cambria* sails are hauled down during the 2006 Régates Royales.

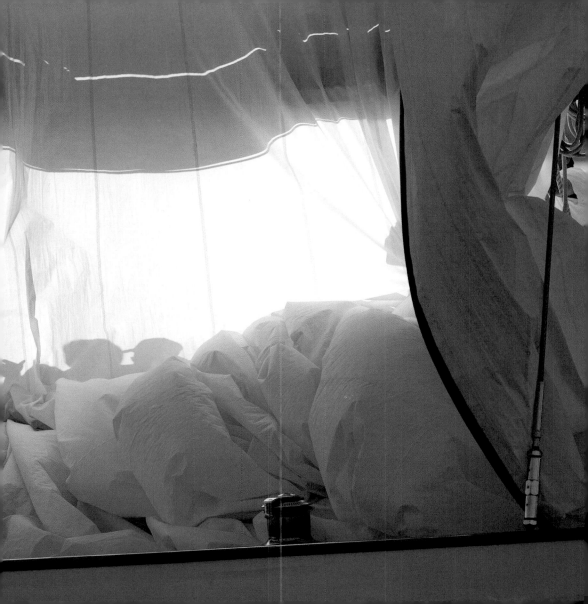

In spite of the long keels and the size of the hull below the waterline, the J-Class yachts seem barely to touch the water (*Shamrock V* is featured in these two pictures).

146 • *Bona Fide*'s mainsail is square to the wind for a fast reach with a following breeze in the 2006 Régates Royales.

147 • In the bows of *Altair*, a sloop dating from 1931, seen during the 2006 Régates Royales.

148-149 • The sun and the sails create beautiful effects off the Isle of Wight during the 2001 America's Cup Jubilee.

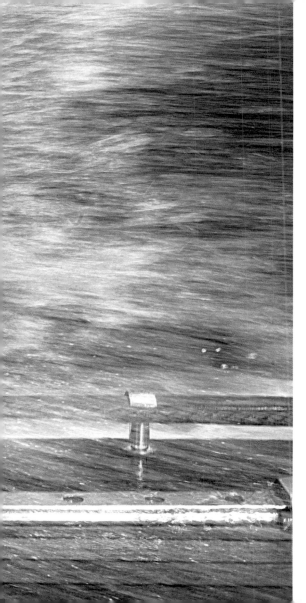

150-151 and 151 • The on-board accessories and instruments are put under great strain: left, during the Superyacht Cup Ulysse Nardin, right, during the 2004 Antigua Classic Week, on *Ranger*.

152-153 • The slim bows of the J-Class *Endeavour* plunges through the waves: this historic yacht is one of only two surviving boats built for the original America's Cup.

A detail and a beautiful head-on shot do justice to the ethereal elegance of *Altair*, a sloop dating from 1931.

156 • *Shamrock V* recalls the fabulous early decades of the twentieth century, when Thomas Lipton heroically attempted to wrest America's Cup from the Americans.

157 • A striking shot of the bow of the modern replica of the J-Class yacht *Ranger* gives an idea of the energy unleashed during a regatta.

● Speed and seaworthiness are often set against each other, but this doesn't seem to apply to these elegant sea swans. The photographs show *Velsheda*, on the left during the 2004 Antigua Classic Week, and on the right off Antigua once again, but five years earlier.

More bows, and busy hands once more: *Velsheda* is shown in action again off Antigua, in 1998 (left) and in 1999. The amount of canvas on these yachts makes it extremely hard work to hoist and haul down the sails.

Antigua, 1999, and *Velsheda* drives through the waves with her customary power.

164-165 and 165 ● Expert professionals are required for some roles, especially in the bows, on classic yachts like *Velsheda* (in these shots taken off Antigua, in 2004 and 2003, respectively).

166-167 ● The complete crew of the *Endeavour* in action on deck during the 1999 Antigua Classic Yacht Regatta.

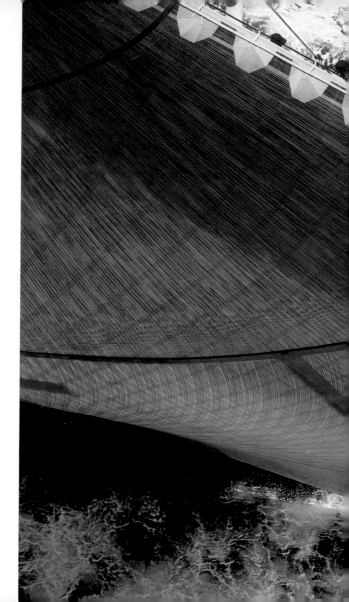

The modern replica of the J-Class yacht *Ranger* sailing in a fresh breeze during the 2005 Antigua Classic Yacht Regatta.

Ranger sailing hard in April 2004, during the Antigua Classic Yacht Regatta.

172 • A beautiful shot captures *Velsheda* off Antigua, in 2004.

172-173 • *Velsheda* leading *Ranger* during the same meeting.

174 • A sail is changed on *Karenita* at
the Saint-Tropez Nioulargue, in 1990.

174-175 • *Karenita* at Saint-Tropez again:
the tapering hulls and large sail area
cause many of the yachts to heel
considerably.

● Two fine pictures of the legendary *Shamrock V* at the Classic Week, as she heads for the open sea off the Principality of Monaco.

◆ A side view and an aerial shot of one of the most beautiful yachts still afloat, the schooner *Shenandoah*, seen here in New Zealand waters.

● *Shenandoah*, dating from 1902, has been described as a "real monument of naval architecture."

The 171 ft (54 m) three masted *Shenandoah* is constantly sailing the the world's seas.

Two spectacular aerial shots pick out the famous *Pen Duick*, the yacht of Eric Tabarly, the French sailor who died in 1998.

● *Mariette* cruising off the Côte d'Azur.
This magnificent yacht, designed by
Herreshoff in 1915, is moored in Antibes.

● Two elegant yachts meet in Italian waters: *Amore Mio* (left) and *Moonbeam* (right) are competing in the Vele d'Epoca regatta off Imperia in 2006.

190 • The fine yawl *Veronique*, launched in 1907, being put through her paces
off Imperia in 2006.

191 • The foresail gets snarled up, captured in an almost sculptural photograph; the action
takes place aboard *Moonbeam* during the Vele d'Epoca regatta off Imperia in 2006.

192 • Overlapping sails at the 2006 Antigua Classic Yacht Regatta.

192-193 • Antigua in 2006 once again: three yachts on the same tack. The first on the left is hauling the wind slightly more than the others.

SETTING a COURSE

The Caribbean in a catamaran. With its low draught, a multihull is the ideal boat for a coral reef.

Setting a Course
Introduction

THOSE WHO ARE NOT USED TO SAILING ARE VERY RESTLESS AT FIRST. THEY GO ABOARD AND ARE SEIZED BY A KIND OF FRENZY. SCURRYING HERE AND THERE, BELOW DECK, ON DECK, IN THE BOWS, IN THE COCKPIT… PERHAPS BECAUSE IT'S CRAMPED. SO MUCH AIR, EVERYWHERE, AND YET… THE THOUGHTS LEADING ONE TO TAKE TO SEA ARE FULL OF DREAMS. A SMOOTH, BLUE EXPANSE; A STEADY, RELIABLE WIND; AN EQUILIBRIUM WHICH NOTHING CAN DISRUPT; DAYS OF FREEDOM, CONTENTMENT WITH THE TRANQUILITY. FOREMOST AT THE MOMENT OF DEPARTURE LOOMS A DESIRE FOR RECONCILIATION: TO GET AWAY FROM THE CITY, AWAY FROM BURDENS, AWAY FROM

- A beautiful cutter-rigged yawl glides over the calm waters of Girolata, in Corsica.

INTRODUCTION Setting a Course

PROHIBITIONS. THE IDEA FORMS OF LOSING ONESELF TO FIND ONESELF, TO DISTANCE ONESELF IN ORDER TO GET CLOSER TO LIFE. THE SEA CONJURES UP ALL OF THIS AND BOATS ARE THE OFFICIATORS IN ITS ANCIENT LITURGY. THEN WISHES BECOME REALITY. THE SHADOW DRIFTING AWAY FROM THE JETTY, AND THUS FROM LAND ITSELF. EVERYTHING CHANGES: THE LAND WAS MORE STABLE; ON BOARD EVERYTHING ROLLS AROUND; THE STOMACH GURGLES A BIT, THE HEAD SPINS; AT EVERY STEP SOME NAMELESS OBJECT TO TRIP OVER; BIG AS THEY MIGHT BE, THE CABINS ARE LIKE HUTCHES COMPARED WITH ROOMS IN A HOUSE; THE SHEETS ARE IMPREGNATED WITH DAMP; THE SALT SWELLS THE FINGERS. NOT BEING ABLE TO GET OFF

INTRODUCTION Setting a Course

THE BOAT BRINGS A COLD SWEAT. AND WHAT ABOUT THE SEA! EVERY NOW AND THEN IT'S A POSTCARD, AND THE REST OF THE TIME IT SULKS, REARS UP AND TURNS NASTY. HOURS OF WAITING, CONFINED TO THE CABIN, ON A SLOW, RELENTLESS ROLLERCOASTER. THE FIRST PORT OF CALL THAT NEVER ARRIVES... AT SEA EVERYTHING IS MORE SHARPLY DEFINED. SETTING OFF LEAVES A BIGGER SCAR. CHANGING IS MORE TRAUMATIC. EXPERIENCING THE WAITING AND THE FEAR IS NOT JUST THE CAUSE OF UN-EASINESS, IT MAKES YOU DEFENSELESS. BUT THOSE WHO HAVE LIVED THROUGH IT KNOW. AFTER A FEW DAYS THE ROLLING SEEMS TO DIMINISH AND SOON IT DIES DOWN. BUT NEVER FEAR, HUNGER WILL RETURN AND SO WILL

Setting a Course
Introduction

THIRST, AND THE EVENING'S PLEASURE WILL MAKE UP FOR THE DAY. THE MEMORY OF LAND WILL VANISH, GIVING WAY TO A RECOLLECTION GOING BACK TO WHO KNOWS WHEN, WHO KNOWS WHERE. TIME, WHICH NEVER PASSES, WILL FLY PAST AND WILL SEEM TO HAVE BEEN THE ONLY REAL TIME. THOSE SAME ANXIETIES WHICH HAD ENGENDERED REGRETS WILL BECOME TEARS OF NOSTALGIA. MORE THAN ANY OTHER INSTANCE OF REAL LIFE, THE SEA PROVIDES HARDSHIPS CONCEALING PLEASURE. DAY AFTER DAY, WAVE AFTER WAVE, IT REVEALS THAT IT IS THE STUFF THAT DREAMS ARE MADE OF: MENDACIOUS AND FLATTERING, BETTER THAN ANY OTHER REALITY.

• Two keen sailors take time out in the bows to relax as their sloop sweeps over the calm sea.

202 ● Martinica. A Privilege 585 sailing
in a good breeze.

202-203 ● Grenadines. Tobago Keys.
A Fontaine Pajot heads
towards the reef.

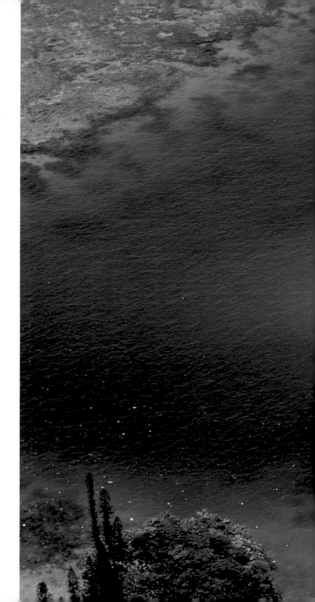

204 • Grenadines. Sailing between reefs and sand in the shallow waters of Tobago Keys.

204-205 • A beautiful sloop anchored inside the reef in the crystal sea of the Grenadines.

206 • A young sailor tries her hand at the tiller of a catamaran.

206-207 • In northern Europe the young learn to sail from an early age, going out in the family boat.

208 • Golden moments: a sailor rests at sunset, with his boat riding at anchor.

208-209 • A light breeze astern and calm sea mean relaxed sailing as the sun goes down.

210-211 • Les Calanques. A fjord. A safe harbor reassures all captains.

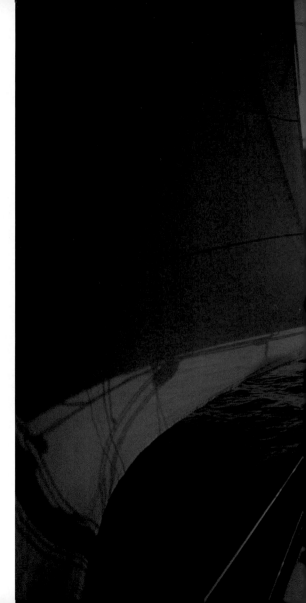

● A yawl coasting past Scandola nature reserve, Corsica.

214 • Bonifacio, Corsica. A catamaran riding at anchor stands out against the turquoise sea.

214-215 • A stiff breeze in Bonifacio: sailing close-hauled, with two hands at the mainsail and a shortened jib.

216-217 • A cutter lying at anchor in the smooth sea of the island of Spargi, in the Maddalena Archipelago, Sardinia.

218-219 • A sail approaching the old mine jetty on one of the Masua cliffs, in Iglesiente, Sardinia.

219 • Rocky shores and inaccessible forelands mean sailing boats are the ideal way of visiting Corsica.

220-221 • A calm sea and a light breeze are indispensable to view these rocks in Sardinia from close up.

222-223 • A sailing boat lying at anchor in Cefalù, bathed in the warm light of a Sicilian sunset.

224-225 ● The Croatian coast is full of natural harbors and bays. Here a boat skims over the calm waters of Telascica Bay, in the Kornati National Park.

225 ● A Venetian tower looms over the main island in the Kornati group.

226-227 ● A caïque lying at anchor in Captain Bay, Turkey.

227 ● A caïque sailing free of danger off a little volcanic island in Turkey.

228-229 ● An original rig on a Maldives boat sailing off the Vabbinfaru atoll, in the North Malé Archipelago.

230 • A catamaran easing between Praslin and Curieuse, in the Seychelles.

230-231 • An ideal anchorage in the Seychelles: the boat lies to leeward of the island of Saint-Pierre and to windward of Curieuse.

The schooner *Shenandoah* sweeping past Noru Hiva, the largest of the Marquesas Islands.

● The Bora Bora lagoon within the
coral reef is the ideal place to explore
with a catamaran.

● The bow of the legendary *Shenandoah* heads towards the coast of Uahine, in the Tuamotu Archipelago.

A catamaran sailing within sight of a small island in New Caledonia, on the edge of the western Pacific.

• The sparkling tongues of sand
of New Caledonia provide a safe
anchorage for sailing boats and
catamarans just a few yards from
the shore and are a paradise
for sailors, snorkelers and
scuba-divers.

242-243 ● Antarctic. Heading for
Port Lockroy, home of the famous
gentoo penguin colonies and
blue-eyed cormorants.

243 ● A shining iceberg floats
by in the Antarctic: the boat
keeps a safe distance.

The ROAR of the SEA

The Roar of the Sea
Introduction

FOR YEARS MAN HAS LIVED WITHOUT KNOWING. SHIPS WEIGHED ANCHOR, AND SOMETIMES NEVER CAME BACK. IT WAS HARD TO CONVEY THE EXPERIENCE OF MOUNTAINOUS SEAS, WITH WAVES AS HIGH AS ANCIENT TREES. IF SOMEONE SAW ONE, HE WAS UNLIKELY TO LIVE TO TALK ABOUT IT. IN THE NINETEENTH CENTURY, SCIENTISTS BEGAN TO SUSPECT WHAT LEGENDS HAD BEEN SAYING FOR MILLENNIA. BUT THEY THOUGHT THAT A ROGUE WAVE MIGHT OCCUR EVERY TEN THOUSAND YEARS. SATELLITES HAVE DONE AWAY WITH ALL THE GLAMOUR OF THIS MYSTERY. THE ESA MAXWAVE PROJECT NOWADAYS RECORDS THE OCCURRENCE OF ROGUE WAVES WITH AMAZING FREQUENCY.

● The fourth leg of the 2002 Volvo Ocean Race. The grinder is hard at work on *Amer Sport One*, in spite of the foul conditions.

INTRODUCTION The Roar of the Sea

NORTH ATLANTIC, 1995: THE *QUEEN ELIZABETH II* IS HIT BY A GIANT WAVE 95 FEET (29 M) HIGH. SOUTH ATLANTIC, 2001: THE CRUISE SHIP *BREMEN* IS SWEPT BY A 98 FT (30 M) WAVE, THE *CALEDONIAN STAR* IS ENGULFED BY A HUGE WAVE ALMOST 132 FT (40 M) HIGH. LETUYA BAY, ALASKA, 1958: PART OF A MOUNTAIN SLIDES INTO THE SEA, CREATING TWO WAVES 1640 FT (500 M) HIGH, WHICH HEAD OFF ACROSS THE OCEAN TO KILL WHO KNOWS WHOM, WHO KNOWS WHERE. ESA KNOWS OF SEVERAL DOZEN LARGE SHIPS THAT HAVE DISAPPEARED AT SEA, SWALLOWED UP BY DEVASTATING WAVES. IN THE PAST FEW YEARS ROGUE WAVES HAVE CAUSED THE LOSS OF 200 SUPERCARRIERS, AND STATISTICS SPEAK OF TWO VESSELS A WEEK SINKING ON ACCOUNT OF ANOMALOUS WAVES. AND YET THE SEA DOES NOT NEED

INTRODUCTION The Roar of the Sea

ANOMALIES TO BE FEARSOME. WHEN I HEAR SOMEONE TALK OF SAILING IN HEAVY SEAS, I GET GOOSE BUMPS ALL OVER. I KNOW AT ONCE WHETHER WHAT HE IS TALKING ABOUT IS TRUE OR IF HE'S MAKING IT UP. I KNOW, BECAUSE LIKE ALL SAILORS, I REMEMBER… WAVES THUNDER, THEY HAVE A VOICE. WHAT CORD CAN VIBRATE IN SUCH A WAY AS TO PRODUCE A ROAR THAT IS SO POWERFUL AND PHYSICAL? THE WIND IN YOUR EARS DEAFENS YOU AND YOU HEAR THE GROWL WHEN THE SEA IS READY TO PLUMMET DOWN ON YOU. IT LIFTS YOU UP, THE WAVE, AS IF THE BOAT WERE A PIECE OF WOOD DEFYING THE FORCE OF GRAVITY. IT BEARS DOWN ON YOU, AND THERE'S NO CHANCE OF SAILING FAST ENOUGH TO GET OUT OF ITS PATH. IT HURLS ITSELF AT YOU BEFORE YOU'RE READY, BATTERING THE BULWARKS, CLIMB-

The Roar of the Sea
Introduction

ING ON DECK. THERE'S NOTHING YOU CAN GRAB HOLD OF, BECAUSE THE WAVE CAN TEAR YOU AWAY FROM ANYTHING. THEN THE BOAT RIGHTS ITSELF. THE WATER POURS OUT OF THE SCUPPERS, AND LEAVES ONE QUESTION HANGING IN THE VOID: "WHAT WILL THE NEXT ONE BE LIKE?" THE FIRST WAVE VAPORIZES A WHOLE MASS OF CERTAINTIES. FROM THAT DAY ON THE SEA HAS A DIFFERENT DENSITY, A DIFFER-ENT SHAPE, A DIFFERENT SMELL. WHILE STILL MOORED AT THE JETTY AND READY TO SET SAIL, YOU LOOK AT THE NIGHT. WHAT DOES THE TONE OF THE WIND'S CHANT TELL YOU? YOU TRY TO GUESS THE ANSWER TO AN ANCIENT QUESTION, ECHOING THE ANXIETIES OF ALL SAILORS THROUGHOUT HISTORY. "WHAT WILL IT BE LIKE OUT THERE?"

- *Assa Abloy* swept by waves. This Swedish boat, designed by Bruce Farr and skippered by Roy Heiner, finished second in the 2001-02 Volvo Ocean Race.

252 ● Southern Brittany on one of those days when any sailor with a little common sense would like to be in port. But Jérémie Beyou, skipper of the monohull *Delta Dore*, thinks otherwise and presses on with his trials.

253 ● The waves give *Delta Dore* no respite. It is dangerous and exhausting to work in the bows in these conditions, even for acrobats of the seas.

• *Delta Dore* off southern Brittany. The sea is extremely rough and life aboard is equally hard.

● A storm at sea. These
are extreme conditions for
Astra, designed by
E. Nicholson and built in
1928 by the Camper &
Nicholson boatyard.

258-259 ● *Delta Dore*'s skipper Jérémie Beyou struggles against heavy seas off Belle-Île-en-Mer, in southern Brittany.

259 ● *Brit Air* in action during the 2006 Transat AG2R, with Le Cleac'h and Troussel on board.

260-261 • *Toshiba*. Heavy seas mean great anxiety for those working in the bows.

261 • It's impossible to stop. The waves are sweeping over the deck, but everything has to be in working order on board.

262-263 • Fourth Act of the 2006 Louis Vuitton Cup. A strong wind.

264 • Jean Luc Van den Heede has a shot at the 1999 Global Challenge, the circumnavigation of the globe against the winds and currents.

265 • Jean Luc sets a record in 2004 of 122 days, 14 hours, 3 minutes and 49 seconds for sailing round the world east-to-west.

266-267 • The sea rears up during the 1993 Nioulargue (subsequently renamed les Voiles de St-Tropez).

267 • A wave crashes down on *VMI*, skippered by Sebastien Josse, while training for the 2002 Route du Rhum.

268 • Sebastien Josse in action during the 2004 Vendée Globe. He sailed round the world single-handed and without making landfall, finishing fifth.

269 • Jean-Pierre Dick manoeuvring his *Virbac* through heavy seas in the 2004 Vendée Globe.

270-271 • The start of the 2005 Transat. In the capable hands of her skipper Yvan Bourbon, the multihull *Brossard* takes on a huge sea.

● A boat disappears into the sea as it careers along at breakneck speed urged on by its spinnaker, during the 2004 Vendée. If it weren't for the starboard handrail, just visible, the crew would be completely submerged by the wave.

274 ● Boats like the monohull *PRB* are built for speed and to take on the heaviest of seas, but not a few criticize this type of race, which pushes men and materials to their limits.

274-275 ● A scene to get the heart racing. Vincent Riou's *PRB* seems about to be swallowed up by the sea in the 2004-05 Route du Rhum.

276 • Michel Dejoyeau's skill is
put to the test in a storm.

276-277 • Tough conditions for
a Swan 56: 55.7 ft (17.53 m)
of boat in the heart of the storm.

278 • The bow is buried in the water during a rough sea crossing.

278-279 • Another spectacular picture: the multihull *Groupama* confronts a seething sea.

280-281 • The boat is in good shape, but the sea is making life extremely hard.

282-283 • *Skandia* facing up to the ocean along the coast of Tasmania, on 28 December 2005. The Sydney to Hobart Race often encounters extremely heavy seas. Here the bow is swallowed up almost to the bowsprit.

284 • The 52 ft (15.8 m) *Yendys* struggling against the sea in the 2005 Sydney to Hobart Race.

285 • "One hand for oneself and one for the boat." The two sailors in the bows seem to illustrate this motto to perfection as they come to terms with mountainous seas in the Sydney to Hobart Race.

● *Pirates of the Caribbean*, skippered by Paul Cayard, sailing in good trim during the 2005-06 Volvo Ocean Race in spite of the pounding waves.

288-289 • *Assa Abloy* in the 2001-02 Volvo Ocean Race. Conditions are worsening and the Swedish hands are shortening the sail.

289 • The considerable amount of sail shortened can be seen after the operation has been concluded.

290 • *Pale Ale Rager* rears up on a wave during the 2003 Sydney to Hobart Race.

290-291 • Titouan Lamazou fights hard in his *Ecureuil d'Aquitaine* in around 50 knots of wind during the 1989-1990 Vendée Globe. He was to finish first.

292 • One of the hands on *Amer Sport One* seems to be walking on water.
His boat is invisible in the trough.

293 • Offshore racing yachts are designed to be able to cleave the waves
with their bow, as in this picture.

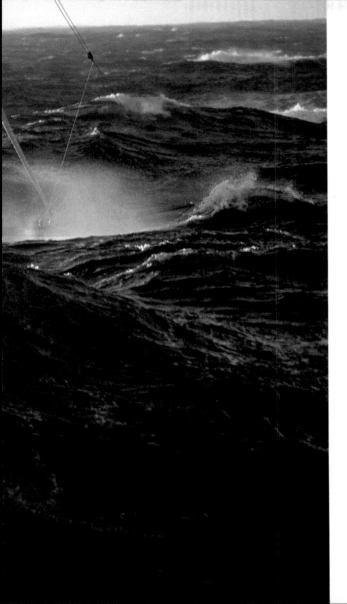

● The trimaran *Géant* disappears behind a wave in the 2002 Route du Rhum. The wind is blowing a stiff 45 knots.

296-297 • Early training in Spain for *ABN Amro 1*. The skipper Mike Sanderson decides to take on a storm to test the boat's handling in rough conditions.

297 • The worse the sea, the better the training gives a taste of what the boats can expect in the Volvo Ocean Race.

298-299 ● *ABN Amro 1* training at Sanxexo (Spain), in October 2005. A wave crashes into the bow to starboard.

299 ● *ABN Amro 1* coming to terms with a rough sea in one of the legs of the 2005 Volvo Ocean Race once again.

300 • *Assa Abloy* on the first, Southampton-Cape Town, leg of the 2001-02 Volvo Ocean Race.

300-301 • The Cape of Good Hope is always sure to greet you with strong winds, mountainous seas and powerful currents. Here, *Assa Abloy* is sailing in good trim while the sea mounts.

Safety precautions are a must on *Assa Abloy* during the second leg of the 2001-02 Volvo Ocean Race. That year's competitors encountered some of the very worst conditions ever.

304-305 • The 2005-06 Volvo Ocean Race: a wave breaks over *ABN Amro 1*'s bow, while the crew are intent on hauling a sail bag along the deck. Anyone not secured by a lifeline is taking a big risk.

305 • This is what the sea is like just 40 miles after the start at Vigo. But the worst is yet to come.

306 • *Illbruck* in action. The yacht
went on to win the 2001-02 Volvo
Ocean Race.

306-307 • The all-female crew
of *Amer Sports Too* bravely
bearing up to very heavy seas
during the Volvo Ocean Race.

Cruising in Australian waters. Sailing with shortened sails, the boat is swallowed up by a wave.

310 • Jean Luc Van den Heede gets to grips with one of the innumerable sticky moments which gave such lustre to his famous 2003-04 record.

311 • Around the world from east to west: one of the toughest challenges man has ever faced, first achieved single-handedly by Joshua Slocum at the end of the nineteenth century. Fighting against the elements on this occasion is Jean Luc Van den Heede.

WINNING at SEA

Palma de Mallorca, 2004, Copa del Rey. Unlike in match races, fleet regattas highlight the skills of the tacticians. Winning depends on finding the wind and working out the best race strategy.

INTRODUCTION Winning at Sea

I WAS ON A FERRY ONE DAY. THE CAPTAIN HAD DE-CIDED TO SAIL IN SPITE OF THE ROUGH SEAS AS HE HAD TO FULFILL A PROMISE: TO TAKE THE BRIDE'S MOTHER TO PON-ZA. HER BROTHER-IN-LAW TO BE WAS A FAMOUS YACHTS-MAN, AND BY COINCIDENCE IT WAS BY SEA THAT HE WAS TO BE REACHED. WHAT AN IDEA, TO GET MARRIED ON AN IS-LAND! AND IN SUCH FOUL WEATHER! THE CAPTAIN HAD HIS WORK CUT OUT TO PREVENT THE BOAT YAWING DANGER-OUSLY, LUFFING AND BEARING AWAY, WITH THE WAVES BREAKING OVER THE BOWS. THE SEA WAS JUST THIS SIDE OF IMPOSSIBLE. ON THE BRIDGE THERE WERE ALSO TWO DECK HANDS AND A COUPLE OF BOYS USED TO COMPETITIVE SAIL-ING. WHEN THE ISLAND OF ZANNONE WAS A FEW MILES DEAD AHEAD, ONE OF THESE LADS ASKED THE CAPTAIN,

INTRODUCTION Winning at Sea

"CAPTAIN, ARE YOU GOING TO PASS ZANNONE TO LEEWARD OR TO WINDWARD?" STRICTLY FROM THE POINT OF VIEW OF THE COURSE, IT WAS A SENSIBLE QUESTION; IT WAS NO FURTHER TO GO ONE SIDE OR THE OTHER. BUT THE SCOWL ON THE CAPTAIN'S FACE SPOKE VOLUMES. IN HIS HEART OF HEARTS HE COULDN'T WAIT TO GET IN THE LEE OF THE ISLAND SO HE COULD HAVE A LITTLE RESPITE. IN A WORD, I HAD BEFORE ME THE DIFFERENCE BETWEEN A MARINER AND A YACHTSMAN. THE FORMER SEEKS SHELTER, AVOIDS GOING WHERE DARK CLOUDS ARE GATHERING, THINKS ABOUT THE BOAT'S TRIM AND DOESN'T CONSIDER THE COURSE OTHER THAN AS A RESULT OF DECISIONS BASED ON SAFETY. HIS CREDO IS FINDING THE RIGHT BALANCE BETWEEN FORCES, CANCELING OUT THE PLANET'S ENERGIES. THE LATTER SEEKS A

INTRODUCTION

CHALLENGE, HE LIKES PRESSURE, AVOIDS ALL PROTECTION, ACTIVELY INVOKES STRONG GUSTS AND IN HIS DREAMS SURFS THE FOAM RIGHT ON THE EDGE OF CAPSIZING. THE FORMER IS FOCUSED ON LEAVING, THE LATTER ON ARRIVING. THE FORMER NEVER MIND LEAVING, THE LATTER ARE SOMETIMES DISAPPOINTED WHEN THEY ARRIVE. EVEN THEIR BOATS ARE DIFFERENT. THE BOAT OF A MARINER WHO LOVES TO CAST OFF HAS A SHORT MAST, A SHELTERED COCKPIT, A SHORT BOOM AND THE WATER LINE SACRIFICED TO LINE. THE BOAT OF SOMEONE YEARNING TO ARRIVE IS HIGHLY STRUNG, WITH POWERFUL ACCESSORIES AND COLORS AND NUMBERS THAT MAKE IT UNIQUE. IT LIES LOW IN THE WATER, AS IF WANTING TO GLIDE OVER THE WATER AT WAVE HEIGHT. ITS MAST AND BOOM SEEM TO DEFY THE LAWS OF NATURE.

INTRODUCTION Winning at Sea

ON BOARD THE FORMER THERE IS A CLUTTER OF HOUSE-HOLD OBJECTS, WHILE THE LATTER IS FREE OF ALL BALLAST. THE RACERS HAVE BEEN BITTEN BY THE BUG OF COMPETI-TION AND THEIR BOATS CHAMP AT THE BIT, THEY QUIVER AND LET OUT A WARRIOR'S CHANT. THEIR HANDLING OF THE BOAT IS GOVERNED BY A SPORTING CODE, WITH PRIORITIES AND PROHIBITIONS. WHEN THEY SAIL THEY TAKE INTO ACCOUNT THE MOVES OF OTHERS ON THE WATER, LIKE THEM, AND OTH-ER BOATS, LIKE THEIRS. THOSE WHO SET SAIL, BY CONTRAST, ARE ONLY ESCAPING FROM THE LAND. THEY HOPE TO HEAL SEPARATIONS AND MAKE GOOD EARLIER NEGLECT, AND IN ORDER TO DO THIS THEY HAVE NO NEED OF A PRECISE COURSE, BUT OF WELCOMING HARBORS. THEY DO WANT TO RETURN, BUT ONLY AFTER A LONG, LONG TIME.

318-319 • The skipper
Vincent Riou during the
2006 Route du Rhum.
Note the boat with
no draft.

320-321 • These
great racing yachts
(in the illustration
VM Matériaux,
skippered by Jean
Le Cam, during the
2006 Route du Rhum)
use state-of-the-art
materials and
technology.

322 • A single-handed sailor like Armel Le Cleac'h (here at the helm of *Brit Air* during the 2006 Route du Rhum) can only take short naps and has to be always at the ready.

323 • *Brit Air* again, during the Route du Rhum: if yachts once used to be oval, narrow in the bows and narrow again in the stern, now they look triangular.

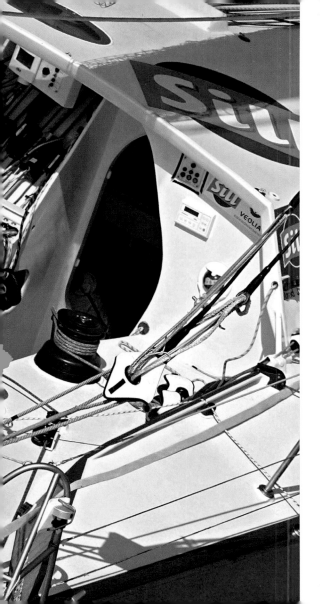

Left, the skipper Roland Jourdain at the coffee grinder of *Sill et Veolia*, as he prepares for the 2006 Route du Rhum. Right, a good view of the canting keel shifted to windward.

The 2006 Route du Rhum: the skipper Jean-Pierre Dick stands up to the waves in the bows of *Virbac Paprel*. Even when the sea is dead calm, the single-handed sailor's life is never easy.

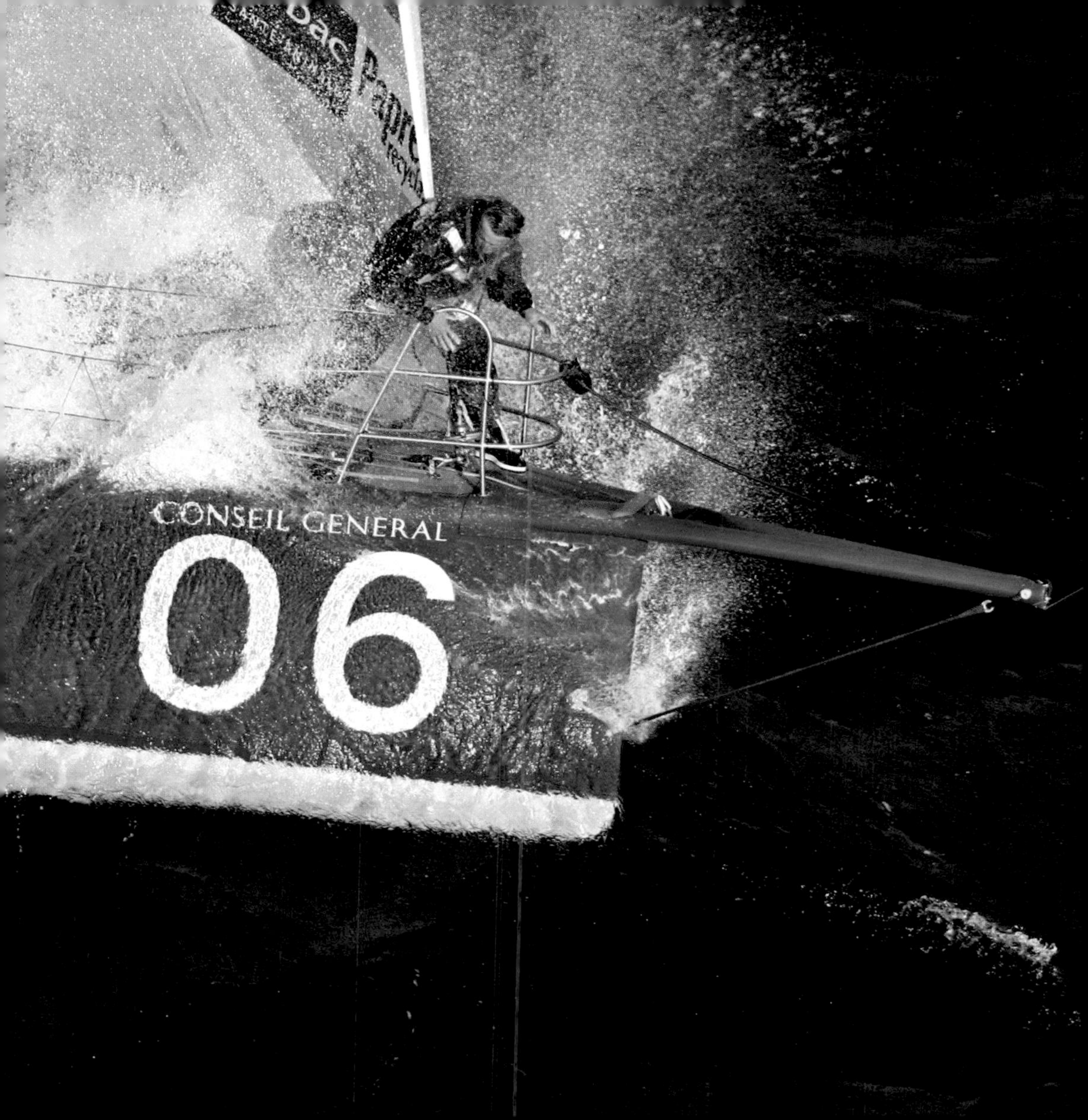
CONSEIL GENERAL
06

328 • Tom Braidwood in the bows of *Ericsson Racing Team* in February 2006, during the Volvo Ocean Race. Being competitive means always looking to improve the boat's trim.

329 • A beautiful aerial shot of *Pirates of the Caribbean*, skippered by Paul Cayard and pictured in May 2006, during the Volvo Ocean Race.

• Even in oceanic
regattas like the Volvo
Ocean Race (known as
the Whitbread Round
the World Race until
1998) there are times
when the wind and sea
conditions are mild.

There seems to be no protection for the crew on offshore racing yachts (pictured here, a Volvo 70 skippered by Grant Whanington getting to grips with the first leg of the Volvo Ocean Race, from Vigo, Portugal, to Cape Town).

334-335 ● An unusual picture. After thousands of miles, two boats are still sailing close together. *Movistar* and *ABN Amro 1* during the 2006 Volvo Ocean Race.

335 ● The Brasilian yacht *Brasil 1* can smell the air of home in the fourth leg of the 2006 Volvo Ocean Race.

336 • The spinnaker, the big sail used to exploit a following wind, is being got ready on board *ABN Amro 1*, one of the competitors in the 2006 Volvo Ocean Race.

337 • *Brasil 1*, skippered by Torben Grael, braves the sea between Vigo and Cape Town, in the 2005 Volvo Ocean Race.

338-339 ● Dead calm for one of the starts on the 2006 Volvo Ocean Race. This was the Melbourne to Wellington, New Zealand, leg.

340-341 ● *Rodeo* on the waves for Ericsson Racing Team, skippered by Neal McDonald, during the first leg of the 2005 Volvo Ocean Race.

The 2005-06 Volvo Ocean Race saw a boat crewed by professional sailors used to launch a Hollywood film for the first time. The skull and crossbones on the sail speaks for itself: it's *Pirates of the Caribbean*, one of a successful series of films starring Johnny Depp.

344 • A beautiful head-on shot of Neal McDonald's boat in the 2005 Volvo Ocean Race.

344-345 • *Brasil 1* speeds towards Cape Town. A calm sea and a blistering pace during the 2005 Volvo Ocean Race.

346 • The powerful *ABN Amro 1*, just after the start of the 2005-06 Volvo Ocean Race. She was to go on to cross the finishing line first.

347 • An unusual shot shows the canting keel of *ABN Amro 1*, in this case photographed during the second leg of the 2005 Volvo Ocean Race, from Cape Town to Melbourne.

348-349 • The 1997-98 Whitbread. On the left *Merit*, skippered by Grant Dalton, who was given the helm of New Zealand off Valencia in 2007.

349 • The 1997-98 Whitbread. Boat designs have evolved enormously since then.

350 • The tough and beautiful Ellen MacArthur in action on Kingfisher during the 2000 Vendée.

351 • The single-handed sailor Sebastien Josse at the coffee grinder during the 2004 Vendée.

● The Volvo Ocean Race (left, the 1996-97 race) is a round-the-world competition over a number of legs and with a full crew, while the Vendée Globe (right, the 2004 race) is non-stop and single-handed.

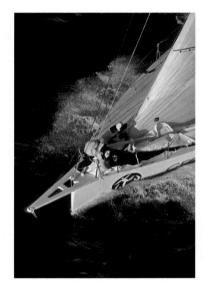

354 • The striking bow of a 1996 offshore racing yacht, shown here during the Vendée.

355 • The engineering concepts behind this type of racing yacht make them look like giant sailing platforms, as illustrated by Hervé Laurent at the 2004 Vendée.

● Two single-handed sailors at the 2004 Vendée Globe: Hervé Laurent (left) and Roland Jourdain. The French are leaders in this field.

358 • Sailing single-handedly or as a pair from Le Havre to Bahia. This is the 2005 Transat Jacques Vabre.

359 • The yellow yacht, *Bonduelle*, and her skipper Jean Le Cam, taking on the sea in the 2004-05 Vendée Globe.

● *Hugo Boss*, the yacht; Alex Thompson, the skipper. The race is the Vendée Globe Open 60, but the real stars, as usual, are the challenging sea and strong wind.

362 ● Le Havre, 5 November 2005: the monohulls starting off on the Transat Jacques Vabre have well over 4000 miles of sea ahead of them.

362-363 ● *Ecover* (United Kingdom-Switzerland) has just set off on her 2005 challenge, the Transat Jacques Vabre, from Le Havre to Ascension, in the mid-Atlantic, and back.

364 • The start of the 2005 Transat Jacques Vabre: stamina and a capacity to take short naps are the two key aptitudes in great ocean crossings such as this.

365 • Start at le Havre, finish at Bahia. *Pro-Form*'s windward rudder is completely out of the water at the start of the 2005 Transat Jacques Vabre.

Yachts at the start of the 2005 Transat Jacques Vabre. One gets used to the sea. But it takes lot of courage to take on heavy seas for weeks on end.

ABN Amro forces her bow through a wave. This is the 2006 Sydney to Hobart and the worst is yet to come.

● Australia to Tasmania, during the 2003 Rolex Sydney to Hobart Race: the wind is fierce and the bow slices into the waves at great speed.

● Yachts competing off Mallacoota, in the Australian State of Victoria, during the 2003 Rolex Sydney to Hobart Race. They seem to be careering along at breakneck speed, but they're actually doing no more than a couple of dozen knots, in the open sea.

374 • The Tasman Sea is a challenging prospect, seen here in the 2003 Rolex Sydney to Hobart Race. The first edition of this classic competition was held in 1945.

375 • This striking aerial shot shows the bow of *Wild Oats XI* cleaving through Australian waters during the 2006 Sydney to Hobart Race.

376-377 • A beautiful summer's day in Australia and the contestants in the 1990 Sydney to Hobart Race are welcomed by the silhouette of Sydney and the sparkling waters of Botany Bay.

378-379 ● Crew maneuvering on a Farr 40, during the 2005 Key West Race Week. This class of boat has a world championship and several events.

380-381 ● The fleet lined up for the start of the 2006 Key West Race.

382 ● The Swann 45 class is beginning to make a name for itself. Here, two boats of this type get ready for the start during the 2005 Key West Race.

383 ● Yachts crossing just a hair's breadth from each other in the 2005 Key West Race.

384-385 ● Key West in 2005: the buoy must be close. The genoa is up and the spinnaker is on its way down.

● The spinnakers are hauled down during the 2004 Key West Race: although they are smaller, the 131 ft (40 m) yachts also boast a sail area large enough to be awkward to handle.

388-389 ● *Aera* skipping over the waves on 16 January 2006, the first day of the Key West event. Florida's waters are a regular port of call in the world sailing circuit.

390-391 ● Day two at Key West: a beautiful picture of this fleet of Swann 45s straining towards the upwind mark.

392-393 ● The 2004 Copa del Rey, Majorca. ITA 2222 identifies Roberto Braida's *Dipende dal Vento*.

Action on board two contenders
in the 2006 Copa del Rey: on the
left, *Movistar*, on the right *Cuor
di Leone*, the Swan owned by
Leonardo Ferragamo, whose
Nautor boatyard builds these
yachts.

The fleet slicing through the waters off Palma de Majorca during the Copa del Rey, in August 2005. It's not easy to see exactly who is in the lead. It depends on where the buoy is at the moment.

A tussle for the lead during the
2004 Maxi Yacht Rolex Cup, in
Porto Cervo. This famous firm has
always supported sailing events:
some of the most spectacular
regattas in the world are organized
by Rolex.

● Two moments in the 2006 Super Yacht Cup held in Palma de Majorca in 2002. Maxi yachts often race together with the monotype classes in the great sailing circuits. A combination of beauty and power that draws admiring glances.

402 • Sardinia, 2006: *Wild Oats* competing in the Maxi Yacht Rolex Cup.

402-403 • A shot from the 2006 Maxi Yacht Rolex Cup: the genoa is ready in the luff groove, ready to change tack.

404-405 • The spectacular venue of Porto Cervo for the 2006 Rolex Cup.

406-407 • The sun plays with the shadows while sails are hoisted in Majorca, on the first day of the Copa del Rey.

408-409 ● The 2007 Superyacht Cup Ulysse Nardin, in Spain: no modern yacht can compete in elegance with a Classic Yacht.

410-411 ● The sails of *Atalanta II* and *Velsheda* sweep behind the rocks at Porto Cervo during the 2006 Maxi Yacht Rolex Cup.

412 ● Sails crossing at the 2006 Barcolana.

412-413 ● A beautiful picture of a blown spinnaker during the 2006 Barcolana, in Trieste. Mistake or tactic to be quicker round the mark?

● An amazing gathering of sails crowding the Gulf of Trieste for the 1998 Barcolana. The sea is almost invisible behind the sails.

The legendary Fastnet Rock, pictured during the 2003 and 2005 Rolex Fastnet Races, left and right respectively: this is a symbolic place for racing yachtsmen throughout the world.

● The 2003 Fastnet Race was the scene of great feats and terrible tragedies. The sea in these parts can be extremely demanding, even for professionals like those pictured.

• The sea mounts and
the 1993 Fastnet Race
enters the critical stage.

422-423 and 423 • The third day in the 2006 Skandia Life Cowes Week, off the Isle of Wight: the sails used with a following wind are big and light, and not easy to control in strong wind conditions.

424-425 • Pictured during Cowes Week in 2006, this yacht's lines are hard to make out, covered as they are by spray.

426 • A fleet of Mumm 30s racing off Dunkirk during the 2006 Tour de France à la Voile. This race has a large following, as does the Giro d'Italia in Vela after years in the doldrums.

426-427 • The 2006 Tour de France à la Voile starts from La Roche Bernard, in Brittany. Racing along the coast has the added charm of seeing one's country from the sea.

428 • A Mumm 30 getting to grips with a leg of the 2006 Tour de France near the Pointe de Toulinguet lighthouse, in Brittany, at the very tip of the Finisterre headland.

428-429 • Another Mumm 30 competition during the 2006 Tour de France à la Voile. The French Atlantic coast offers some spectacular scenery. The lighthouses of Normandy and Brittany are famous throughout the world.

The yachts racing in the 2006 Tour de France à la Voile sail past the Phare de la Vieille, renowned for being an especially isolated spot on the dangerous Brittany coast.

432 and 432-433 ● Left, the bows are lined up ready for the start of the 2006 Tour de France à la Voile; right, after the start on the Camaret to La Roche Bernard leg.

434-435 ● The crew of the British skiff *Radii* at work during the 2006 JJ Giltinan Trophy, in Sydney. Skiffs are increasingly popular lighweight boats, with wings and trapeze, large sail area and carbon-fiber masts.

• With no bulb to right the boat and sails that are extremely large for such a light craft, sailors constantly have to shift position to find the right balance (left, *SX Projects*; right, *Velamare*, at the 2006 JJ Giltinan Trophy).

● Skiffs gliding over the river Swan, in Perth, Australia, during the 2004 World Championship for this class.

● The small sails of the Laser Class doing battle at Hyères during the 2004 Semaine Olimpique Française de Voile (SOF).

442 ● The crew in action aboard a Star Class boat during the 2006 Rolex Baltic Week

442-443 ● Waves crossing in Gaeta, where Star Class boats compete during the 2004 World Championship.

444 • Young sailors during the 2006 World Youth Championships at Martigues, near Marseilles.

445 • Racing for Olympic laurels at Athens, in 2004.

446-447 • A parade of blue sails announces the fleet competing for the 2002 World Sailing Games organized by ISAF (International Sailing Federation).

Female crews competing in the 470 Open World Championships at Hyères, in 2003 (left), and at the 2002 World Sailing Games, in Marseilles.

WHEN PLACE
there is no
second

The bow of *Alinghi*, and in the background the New Zealand entry, in 2007.

INTRODUCTION

THE ENGLISH MAY HAVE INVENTED IT, BUT THEY HAVE NEVER WON THE AMERICA'S CUP. IT WAS FIRST COMPETED FOR A LONG TIME AGO IN 1851, ON THE SOLENT, WHICH IS THE STRETCH OF SEA SEPARATING THE ISLE OF WIGHT FROM ENGLAND'S SOUTH COAST. PRINCE ALBERT PRESIDED OVER THE RUNNING OF THE EXHIBITION, WHICH WAS HELD TO CELEBRATE TECHNOLOGICAL PROGRESS AND THE EXPANSION OF THE BRITISH EMPIRE. ALBERT INVITED THE AMERICANS TO SEND A BOAT OVER AS AN EXAMPLE OF THE STANDARDS REACHED BY THEIR BOAT-BUILDERS. THE COMMODORE OF THE NEW YORK YACHT CLUB, ONE JOHN COX STEVENS, SENT A SCHOONER CALLED *AMERICA*. THIS BOAT WAS USED TO RACE TO BIG SHIPS LYING AT ANCHOR

INTRODUCTION When there is no Second Place

OFFSHORE – THE FIRST TO REACH SUCH A SHIP WOULD SE-CURE THE RIGHT TO UNLOAD HER. THE CREW WAS A BIT ROUGH AND READY, PUTTING SUBSTANCE BEFORE APPEAR-ANCE. THEY CROSSED THE ATLANTIC AND ENTERED THE SO-LENT, WHERE THEY PROCEEDED TO TACK BACK AND FORTH: THEY WOULD APPROACH A BOAT, LAUNCH A CHALLENGE AND RACE. THERE WAS NO NEED FOR BUOYS. IT WAS EASY TO SEE WHO WAS THE FASTER. "THERE'S THE FINISH. WE'VE WON." WELL, ON THAT DAY THERE WAS A FRESH NORTH-WESTERLY BLOWING ABOUT 15 KNOTS AND NOT A SINGLE ENGLISH BOAT COULD KEEP UP WITH THE AMERICAN DOCK WORKERS. IT GOT TC THE POINT WHERE YACHTS STOPPED LEAVING HARBOR TO AVOID GETTING EGG ON THEIR FACES.

INTRODUCTION When there is no Second Place

THE HEADLINES THE DAY AFTER LAID IT ON WITH A TROWEL: "NO ONE TO MATCH OUR COUSINS FROM ACROSS THE POND." NO, THAT JUST WOULD NOT DO! THE ROYAL YACHT SQUADRON COULD NOT JUST SIT BACK AND TAKE THAT HUMILIATION. SO THEY DARED THE *BARBARIANS* TO TAKE PART IN THE HUNDRED GUINEA REGATTA – ONCE ROUND THE ISLE OF WIGHT, WITH THE NATION'S HONOUR AT STAKE. AND THROWING CAUTION TO THE WINDS, *AMERICA* ACCEPTED. ON AUGUST 22 1851 THEY SAILED OUT OF THE HARBOR AND FOUND 14 CLIPPERS WAITING, THE FLOWER OF THE ENGLISH SAILING WORLD. AT A CERTAIN POINT QUEEN VICTORIA, WHOSE EYESIGHT WAS POOR, ASKED A RETAINER, "WHO IS FIRST?", TO WHICH CAME THE CALM REPLY, "AMERICA,

INTRODUCTION When there is no Second Place

MA'AM." "AND WHO IS SECOND?" "MA'AM, THERE IS NO SECOND." FROM THAT DAY THEIR CUP WAS GIVEN THE NAME OF THE VICTOR, AMERICA, AND THE POOR ENGLISH NEVER WON IT. EVEN THE STUBBORN SCOT SIR THOMAS LIPTON NEVER MANAGED IT, ALTHOUGH HE MADE FIVE ATTEMPTS OVER SOME 30 YEARS. EVENTUALLY EVEN THE AUSTRALIANS HAD A GO. ANOTHER BUSINESSMAN, ALAN BOND, WENT SO FAR AS TO GO TO NEW YORK WITH A SPANNER AND SAID HE WOULD PRISE THE CUP FREE AND CARRY IT OFF. THERE WERE A NUMBER OF CONTENDERS THAT YEAR AND THE LOUIS VUITTON CUP WAS CREATED AS A RESULT. ONE OF THE CONTENDERS WAS *AZZURRA*, WHICH FINISHED THIRD. BOND WON AND FOR THE FIRST TIME THE CUP DID NOT RETURN TO

When there is no Second Place

THE STATES. THEN IT WAS THE NEW ZEALANDERS WHO TRIED TO CLAIM IT, TURNING UP IN SAN DIEGO WITH A BOAT NEARLY 120 FT (37 M) LONG. THE AMERICANS SUCCESSFULLY DEFENDED THE CUP THEY HAD WON BACK WITH A CATAMARAN JUST 59 FT (18 M) LONG. BUT THE KIWIS KNEW IT WAS JUST A MATTER OF TIME; THEIR TURN WOULD COME SOON ENOUGH. FIRST, THEY WERE TO TAKE THE CUP TO AUCKLAND ON TWO HOME-BUILT BOATS, THEN THEY CARRIED IT TO EUROPE IN A SWISS BOAT. THE WORLD CHANGES: NOWADAYS A VESSEL STUFFED FULL OF KIWIS CAN BE DESCRIBED AS A SWISS BOAT. THAT IS WHAT BEING MODERN MEANS. ANYONE WHO THINKS OTHERWISE IS LIVING IN THE PAST.

● *Areva Challenge* in the 2007 Louis Vuitton Cup. After dominating in the big offshore regattas, the French found life harder in the match race format.

458-459 • *Victory Challenge*, the Swedish entry, was in the leading group in the 2007 Louis Vuitton Cup.

459 • *China Team* gave the Chinese their first taste of competition in the 2006 Louis Vuitton Cup, ably reinforced with French expertise.

460 • *Alinghi* in training.

460-461 • *Luna Rossa*, flying the colors of the Genoese Yacht Club Italiano, shown training in the waters off Valencia.

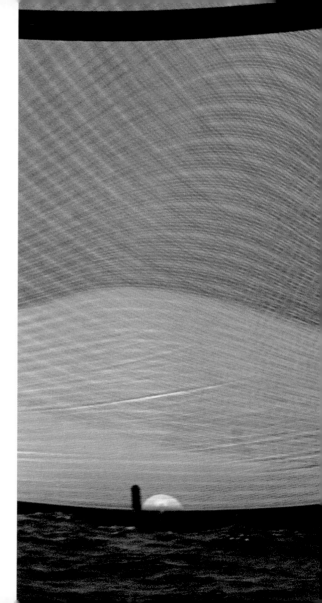

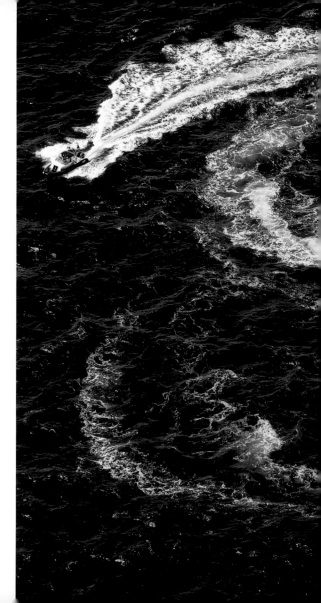

462 ● June 2007, Valencia: *Luna Rossa* and *ETNZ* avoid touching, but collisions are not rare in America's Cup racing.

462-463 ● The New Zealanders dominated the final of the 2007 Louis Vuitton Cup against *Luna Rossa*.

464 ● Acrobats in the bows: the crew of
the New Zealand boat *Emirates*, during
the final of the 2007 Louis Vuitton Cup.

464-465 ● And acrobats at the
masthead, once again on *Emirates*
in 2007.

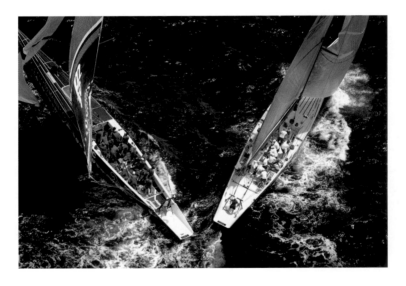

466 • Frenchmen (crewing *K-Challenge*) against South Africans (crewing *Shosholoza*) clash for the first time in America's Cup races, in 2007.

467 • *Luna Rossa*'s bow is outlined against the hull of *K-Challenge* during Act 3 of the 2007 Louis Vuitton Cup in Valencia.

468 • The chasing boat enjoys the best of the conditions in the downwind leg, surfing on the leading boat's wash and stealing its wind.

469 • A sail in the water slows a boat down. Here, *+39* loses her gennaker in Act 2 of the 2007 Louis Vuitton Cup.

470 • The moment when *K-Challenge* "blows" her spinnaker.

471 • *Alinghi* tears her spinnaker in Marseilles in 2005, Act 1 of the Louis Vuitton Cup.

472 • One of the Acts of the 2005 Louis Vuitton Cup took place in the cold waters off Malmö.

473 • *Alinghi*, *Le Défi* and *Luna Rossa* crossing during Act 3 of the 2004 Louis Vuitton Cup, in Valencia.

474 ● *Luna Rossa* and *Desafio Español* virtually within touching distance of each other at the 2005 Louis Vuitton Cup.

475 ● *Desafio Español*, Trapani 2005: the crew have their hands full in the bows of the Spanish boat.

476-477 ● *+39* in action during Act 8 of the 2005 Louis Vuitton Cup, held at Trapani.

478 • The bow of the Italian *Luna Rossa* bursts through a wave.

478-479 • Swedes against New Zealanders: a clash that matches different schools of sailing.

● Fleet regattas. Their sheer size and elegance makes these yachts an awesome sight for fans. In these pictures: left, rounding a mark; and right, the fleet in action in Act 1 of the 2004 Louis Vuitton Cup, held at Marseilles.

● *Oracle* plowing the waves off Marseilles in training, in 2004.

Fly Emirates
TOYOTA
www.emirates.com
NEW ZEALAND
Fly Emirates

484-485 ● *Alinghi* and *Emirates* jostling for position off Marseilles during the 2004 Louis Vuitton Cup.

485 ● A fleet regatta, Act 1 of the 2004 Louis Vuitton Cup.

Act 1 of the 2004 Louis Vuitton Cup: the genoa is stowed away after hoisting the spinnaker. *Alinghi* has clearly just rounded the upwind mark.

- The New Zealand crew at work.
New Zealand has supplied the
most sailors in America's Cup
racing over the past decade.
It should be remembered that
many of the crew on *Alinghi* were
also from New Zealand.

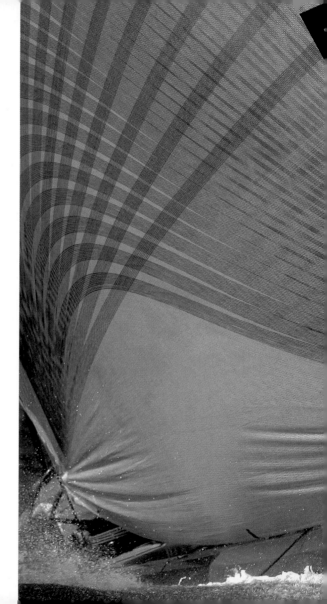

• *Alinghi* and *Oracle* in a close-fought duel during the 2004 Louis Vuitton Cup. The picture shows how the carbon-fiber blend varies according to the section of sail.

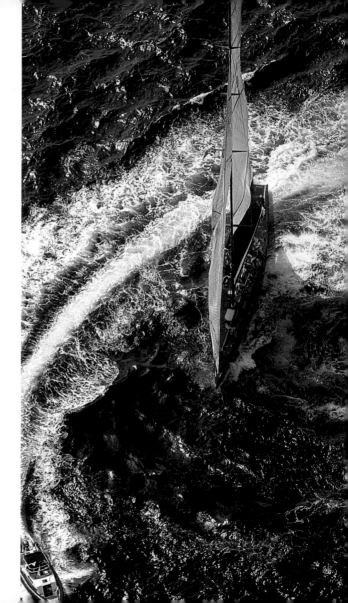

• *Le Défi*, *Shosholoza*
and *K-Challenge* in
Act 1 of the 2004 Louis
Vuitton Cup.

● The start of the Louis
Vuitton Cup, during the
2007 America's Cup:
from right to left, *Areva
Challenge* (France),
Oracle (USA),
Shosholoza (South
Africa) and *Victory
Challenge* (Sweden).

• The budget is hugely important
in America's Cup racing, but even
more crucial are axperience
and the time necessary to
develop the boats.

498-499 and 499 • A direct faceoff between *Emirates* and *BMW Oracle* during Act 12 of the 2006 Louis Vuitton Cup, off Valencia. A boat's chances of winning depend 51% on the upwind leg.

500-501 • *Emirates*, in the right foreground, and *BMW Oracle* in a cloud of spray off Valencia in 2006. It's a hard life for the bowmen.

502 • The crew keeps low during the upwind leg so as not to spoil the yacht's aerodynamics and slow her down (here *Luna Rossa* in the 2006 Louis Vuitton Cup).

503 • James Spithill in action with *Luna Rossa*, in Valencia, during the 2006 Louis Vuitton Cup. The young Australian became a real hero, forcing the Americans on *Oracle* to concede two penalties in the build-up to the start of one of the semi-final races. It had never happened before.

504 and 504-505 • Two gennakers are "blown" on *Emirates Team New Zealand* and *Alinghi*.

506-507 • Valencia, America's Cup Act 4. Dean Barker at the leeward helm on Emirates Team New Zealand.

508 • In the semi-final, *BMW Oracle* rounded every mark of the five races behind *Luna Rossa*.

508-509 • Head to head in the run up to the start.

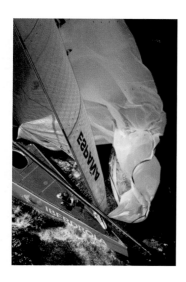

Desafío Español. The hosts were surprisingly quick, thanks too to their helmsman Karol Jablonski.

512-513 • A perfect sea for the final duel between *Emirates* and *Desafio Español* during the semi-final of the 2007 Louis Vuitton Cup, off Valencia.

513 • The first match-up in the semi-final of the 2007 Louis Vuitton Cup, on 14 May. The 18th man aboard *Desafio Español*, in the orange top, is none other than King Juan Carlos de Borbón of Spain.

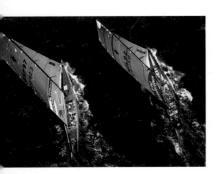

514 and 514-515 ● A very close-fought semi-final. The Spanish "went down fighting" against the Kiwi champions.

516-517 ● They're off. The yachts hurtle towards the start line at the end of the countdown.

The crowds, all cheering for the three Italian boats, were one of the features of Act 8 of the 2007 Louis Vuitton Cup, at Trapani.

● *Luna Rossa* manoeuvering. The Australian James Spithill is at the helm.

● Tightrope-walkers.
Mascalzone Latino's
bowman works on the
windward end of the
spinnaker pole hanging
over the sea.

- Having a man at the masthead is very fashionable in the America's Cup.

526 ● Dean Barker and his
crewmates aboard *Emirates*
during the 2007 Cup.

526-527 ● Fourth day of racing
during the final of the 2007
America's Cup. *Alinghi* prepares
to round the mark.

528 • The boats circle behind the start line as they try to secure the best position for the off.

528-529 • *Alinghi* recovers her spinnaker.

Anxious moments. The *Emirates Team New Zealand* bowman goes overboard during a race in Valencia.

● Second day of racing in the final of the 2007 America's Cup. *Emirates Team New Zealand* wins and draws level with *Alinghi*: 28 seconds the lead at the finish.

Alinghi versus *Emirates*: it's many years since there has been such a closely contested final. The 32nd America's Cup saw frequent and astonishing turnarounds and twists of fate.

536 • An emblematic image.
One of *Alinghi*'s crewmen with his hands
on the symbol of the Cup.

536-537 • Boats are hardly ever far
apart in a match-race. In the 2007 Cup
event the exact opposite was true.

NZL 92
www.newzealand.com
NEW ZEALAND
OMEGA
Estrella Damm
NEW ZEALAND

538 • Dean Barker, New Zealand's helmsman, was often the most aggressive in the pre-start circling maneuvers.

538-539 • One of the key moments of the final. New Zealand tears her spinnaker and is forced to hoist a fresh one immediately.

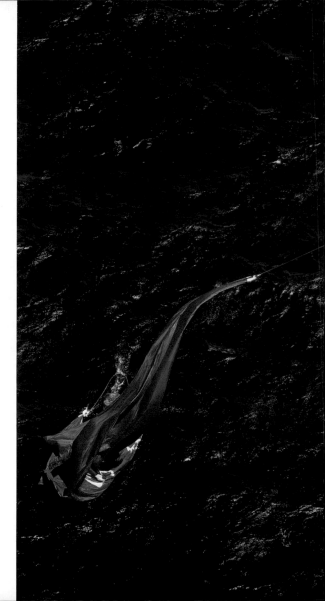

540 ● The bowman at the very tip of the bow. This is his normal position at the start of the race.

540-541 ● In the 2007 Cup, held at Valencia, the *Alinghi* team proved once again able to carry out maneuvers extremely smoothly.

New Zealand, the challenger, was often ahead in Valencia, as in these pictures.

544 • The New Zealand and Swiss boats were very evenly matched when sailing at full speed.

544-545 • More circling before the start.

546-547 • *Alinghi* breaks the dial-up, in which the boats are motionless side by side, bows to the wind, and tries to escape to port.

547 • The two yachts on the layline, the shortest route to the upwind mark.

548-549 • Early June 2007. The spinnaker is dropped on New Zealand during one of the races against *Luna Rossa*.

550-551 • *Alinghi* has already rounded the downwind mark. New Zealand is trailing.

net

● *Alinghi* was always the pre-race favorite. While not having things all her own way, she did not disappoint.

Fourth race of the final. Ed Baird and his crew win and draw level with *Emirates Team New Zealand* at two wins each.

556 • The eighteenth man is in the bows. He can't talk or touch anything, but everyone would like to be in his place.

556-557 • A crew practices for years every day to perform smoothly and infallibly.

The Italians of *Luna Rossa* and her great helmsman James Spithill crushed the Americans in their semi-final.

- Moments of glory. *Alinghi* wins America's Cup in Valencia on 3rd July 2007. Ernesto Bertarelli kisses the trophy.

TWIN HULLS

● *Hydroptère* at speed. This boat recorded a world record of 44.81 knots over 1640 ft (500 m) on 4th April 2007.

Twin Hulls
Introduction

WHEN I WENT ABOARD A CAT FOR THE FIRST TIME, I LOOKED AROUND RATHER LOST. WE WERE AT ANCHOR AND COMPLETELY STILL. I MEAN, AS STILL AS ON DRY LAND, WITHOUT EVEN THE SLIGHTEST HINT OF A ROLL. HOW COULD IT BE?

THAT EVENING WE SET SAIL AND I QUICKLY STOWED AWAY THE BOTTLE OF WINE LEFT ON THE TABLE. "WHY ARE YOU PUTTING THAT AWAY?" ASKED THE SKIPPER. THE BOTTLE STAYED ON THAT TABLE FOR TWO DAYS AT SEA WITHOUT EVER FALLING OVER. I WAS IMPRESSED…

THE FIRST MULTI-HULL IN HISTORY SEEMS TO HAVE BEEN 105 FT (32 M) LONG. IT WAS CHINESE AND IT WAS BUILT IN

- *Hydroptère* is lifted by the force of the wind. Amazingly, the original designs for this extraordinary craft built for speed date from 1869.

INTRODUCTION Twin Hulls

THE SIXTH CENTURY AD. IN THE FAR EAST THEY WERE AL-
READY MAKING CLINKER SHIPS IN 2000 BC. THEY WERE
VERY ADVANCED IN NAUTICAL MATTERS, BUT THEY WERE
NOT ALONE.

GREAT EXPLORERS LIKE WALLIS, BYRON, CARTERET AND
COOK TOOK HOME FROM THE PACIFIC THOUSANDS OF
DRAWINGS OF MULTI-HULLED VESSELS, EVEN THOUGH MA-
GELLAN WAS THE FIRST WHITE MAN TO SET EYES ON POLY-
NESIAN CANOES, IN 1521. HE HAD A VERY POOR OPINION OF
THEM, CRITICIZING THEIR LOW FREEBOARD, THEIR RUDI-
MENTARY RIG AND GENERAL FRAGILITY. BUT IN 1799 CAP-
TAIN JAMES WILSON WROTE: *"IT IS AN EXTRAORDINARY
FACT THAT, WITHOUT THE USE OF IRON, RULERS OR PRO-
TRACTORS, AND WITH ONLY A GOOD AXE, THE BONE OF A*

INTRODUCTION Twin Hulls

DEAD FOE AS AN AWL AND CORAL AS A PLANE, THEY CAN HEW A BOAT SO PRECISELY AND SMOOTH IT SO FINELY." THE PEOPLES OF THE PACIFIC SAILED IN THEIR BI-TRIMA- RANS FROM POLYNESIA TO THE EASTERN PART OF THE INDIAN OCEAN, FROM MELANESIA TO MICRONESIA AND FROM THE NORTHERN ATOLLS TO EASTER ISLAND. SO- ME SAY THEY EVEN REACHED CHILE AND COVERED THE WHOLE OF THE PAC FIC. NOT BAD FOR SAILORS MAGEL- LAN REGARDED AS AMATEURS. THE HUGE BUT STILL RU- DIMENTARY MULTI-HULLS OF THE FABULOUS EASTERN SEAS AND THE BOATS OF THE BRAVE POLYNESIANS DO NOT HAVE MUCH IN COMMON WITH SOPHISTICATED MODERN YACHTS BUILT FOR SPEED, EXCEPT THAT THEY ARE ALL BOATS WITH MORE THAN ONE HULL. FIVE HUN-

Twin Hulls

DRED YEARS AGO IT TOOK 79 DAYS TO CROSS THE ATLANTIC. THE SKIPPER WAS CALLED CHRISTOPHER COLUMBUS AND HE WAS IN COMMAND OF A FLEET OF THREE RATHER RUN-DOWN, SINGLE-HULLED SHIPS. ON 13 JANUARY 2007 A BOAT STRUCK LAND WHICH HAD TAKEN JUST 14 DAYS TO MAKE THE CROSSING (14 DAYS, 17 HOURS AND 52 MINUTES, TO BE PRECISE). THE SKIPPER'S NAME WAS MATTEO MICELI AND HIS BOAT WAS A 20 FT (6 M) CATAMARAN: *BIONDINA NERA*. THE GREAT GENOESE, ONE OF THE LEGENDARY FIGURES OF SAILING, WOULD HAVE BEEN LEFT SPEECHLESS. PERHAPS HE MIGHT EVEN HAVE ENVIED HIM.

- Ellen MacArthur, in her *B&Q Castorama*, broke the record in her solo round-the-world race (21,760 miles/35,020 km), finishing in February 2005.

570-571 • The trimaran ORMA 60 *Primagaz* in the Route du Rhum in 1998.

571 • Fécamp Grand Prix. 2002 ORMA Multihull Championship. One of the competing trimarans shows a turn of speed sailing close-hauled.

572 • The crew training on board the 33-metre maxi catamaran *Orange*, a famous record-breaker in the circumnavigation of the globe.

573 • Yvan Bourgnon on board his trimaran in the 2006 Route du Rhum.

Soldini and Malingri on board *TIM Progetto Italia* during the 2005 Transat Jacques Vabre. Extremely strong winds over the whole first leg were forecast before the start, unfortunately proved correct, with a high number of retirements and accidents.

576 • Yvan Bourgnon training on his trimaran in 2006 before the Route du Rhum. Here, *Brossard*'s bow plunges straight into a wave.

577 • Steve Ravussin training on *Orange Project* before the 2006 Route du Rhum.

- Soldini on board T*IM Progetto Italia* at the start of the Transat Jacques Vabre. The yacht was to capsize a few days later, 500 miles (804 km) south of Dakar.

A torn mainsail in the upwind leg at the start of the 2005 Transat, one of the toughest races in the world.

582 • The Swiss Steve Ravussin on board *Orange Project*, in 2006.

582-583 • *Sodebo* leaves Le Havre on 5th November 2003 to race in the Transat Jacques Vabre.

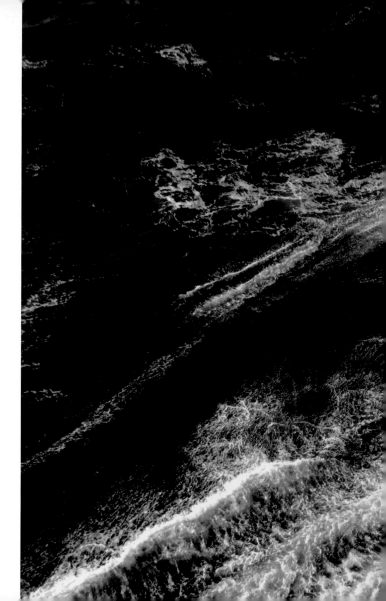

584-585 ● The 60 ft (18.2 m) multihull *Groupama* pictured at the start of the Transat Jacques Vabre, on 5th November 2003. She was to come in first twelve days later, skippered by Franck Cammas.

586-587 ● *Hydroptère*, skippered by Alain Thébault, in Quiberon Bay, in June 2005.

588 • *Hydroptère* practising "skipping" over the water.

588-589 • Alain Thébault's *Hydroptère* sets a new record of 41.69 knots over a nautical mile, as well as setting the record of 44.81 knots over 1640 ft (500 m), on 4th April 2007.

590-591 • The stresses that multihulls have to withstand are truly astonishing. Here Yvan Bougnon tries to do his best after an accident to *Yprema* during the 1998 Transat.

591 • *Yprema* sailing before the accident in 1998.

592 • Michel Desjoyeaux
on *Géant* at Marseilles, where
he won the Café Ambassador
Grand Prix.

592-593 • *Géant*'s bows climb
while Michel Desjoyeaux prepares
to change sails at Trapani in 2006.

594-595 • *Groupama* heeling
slightly owing to her great speed,
during the 2006 Multi Cup 60,
off Trapani.

The start of the 2005 ORMA Championship, at Vigo.

598-599 • *Gitana 11*, designed
in 2001 by Marcvan Peteghem
and Vincent Lauriot-Prévost,
seems to fly off the surface
of the sea off Portimao, in 2006.

599 • From Maxis to Minis.
The 18-foot New Zealand *CT
Sailbattens* accelerates away,
with Phil Airey at the helm.

600-601 • Steve Ravussin training in his 60-foot *Orange Project*.

601 • Reducing the mainsail and staysail is not enough to hold back *Orange Project*.

602-603 • The small "cats" have thousands of fans among sailors. But physical strength and agility are just as important as the wind.

604 • *Banque Populaire* sailing
in good trim over a calm sea.

604-605 • *Trinitaine* practising
maneuvers before the start
of Les Sable d'Olonne.

606 ● In spite of their stability, the big ORMA trimarans achieve such high speeds that the sails have to be shortened considerably, as in this shot of *Fujicolor*.

607 ● The 2001 Jules Verne Trophy. A striking shot of *Orange 1*.

Around the world in 80 days. No challenge could be more alluring. This was the origin of the Jules Verne Trophy. *B&Q Castorama* at the start at Brest, in 2002.

610 ● *Fujifilm* "takes off" as her hull comes almost completely out of the water.

610-611 ● Fujifilm during the 2002 Course des Phares. She was to win the race with Loic Peyron at the helm.

612 • One of the competitors in the 2002 Route du Rhum crosses the finishing line in Guadeloupe.

612-613 • *Groupama* during the 2003 Lorient Grand Prix (Lorient-Fastnet-Lorient).

614-615 ● *Belgacom* (later *Gitana 11*) hurtling along in the 2003 Lorient Grand Prix. Her skipper is Jean-Luc Nélias.

615 ● *Club Med*, a development of the winner of the dramatic The Race, the circumnavigation of the world at high latitudes, in 2001. *Orange* finished second. New speed records are excitingly set day after day.

616 ● Plymouth. Steve Ravussin unleashes his trimaran *Banque Covefi* in the 2004 Transat.

616-617 ● *Club Med* sailing at full speed in 2000 in order to qualify for the regatta of regattas: The Race. The skipper, Bruno Peyron claims to have performed "outrageously" hard maneuvers between Cadiz and San Salvador.

The trimarans sweep past Cagliari, during the 2003 Gran Premio del Campionato ORMA dei Multiscafi.

620-621 • *Sergio Tacchini*, skippered by Karine Fauconnier, in the 2004 Transat. She was to finish fifth, ahead of *Banque Populaire*, *TIM Progetto Italia* and *Sopra Group*.

622-623 • *Sergio Tacchini*'s power is reined in by the toughness and determination of the beautiful Karine Fauconnier.

624-625 • Bruno Peyron's
Orange on the water.

625 • Bruno Peyron sailed
Orange to victory in the 2005
Jules Verne Trophy. He is pictured
here at the finish, at Brest.

626 ● *Playstation*'s foresails
are dropped to cope with
the strong winds.

626-627 ● Strong winds and
a heavy sea make this cat heel
over dangerously.

● Sails are dropped
on the Maxi catamaran
Orange, skippered
by Bruno Peyron, holder
of several records
and organizer in 2000
of the demanding
circumnavigation
The Race.

- The 60 ft (18.2 m)
trimarans competing
in the 2006 Fécamp GP
get to grips with a stiff
breeze in front
of the port. A genoa
is stowed away on
Géant and a staysail
takes its place.

● A thrilling dogfight
between *Groupama*
and *Séant* at Fécamp,
in 2006.

634-635 • *Groupama* reaches
the mark in the Fécamp GP,
on 9th September 2006.

635 • Groupama off Plymouth,
on 31st May 2004.

636 ● *TIM Progetto Italia* is lifted by a strong gust of wind, on a starboard tack off Calvi, Corsica, in 2005.

636-637 ● A spectacular shot of a trimaran being lifted off the water during the 2005 Tour of Corsica.

638-639 ● *Gitana 11* at the Marseilles GP, during the 2006 Multi Cup 60 Café Ambassador.

On the WINGS of BEAUTY

- In 1984 *Nippon Maru*, the Japanese merchant marine training ship, replaced the sailing ship of the same name launched in 1930.

On the Wings of Beauty
Introduction

WHEN THE WISP OF SMOKE CAME OUT OF THE FUNNEL OF THE FIRST STEAMSHIP, SOMEONE ON THE JETTY REMARKED: "THE DAYS OF SAIL ARE OVER."

THE SAME THING HAPPENED WITH TELEVISION, WHICH WAS SUPPOSED TO KILL OFF RADIO, OR WITH THE TELEPHONE ("PEOPLE WON'T SPEAK FACE TO FACE ANY MORE"), OR WITH E-MAIL, WHICH WAS GOING TO MAKE POST OFFICES REDUNDANT. AT EVERY STEP HE TAKES, MAN THINKS EVERYTHING IS GOING TO CHANGE. BUT IT DOESN'T.

NOWADAYS, SAILING SHIPS WITH SEVERAL MASTS OR MAXI CRUISING OR RACING YACHTS ARE MAKING A

• *Sagres*, launched in Hamburg in 1936, has fulfilled many functions over the years, the last of which was as the Portuguese navy training ship.

INTRODUCTION On the Wings of Beauty

COMEBACK. WHEN WAS A SAILING SHIP EVER SOME-THING THE PETTY BOURGEOIS COULD ASPIRE TO IN THE EIGHTEENTH CENTURY? THEY NO LONGER CARRY CAR-GO, IT'S TRUE, BUT THIS CERTAINLY DOES NOT HAMPER THEIR DEVELOPMENT. SPECIAL EVENTS, TOURIST CHAR-TERS AND BIG COMPETITIONS CONTINUE TO ATTRACT CORPORATE INTEREST AND TO DRAW PEOPLE FROM BOATYARDS, ENTHUSIASTS AND JUST PLAIN JOE PUB-LIC. IF THE *AMERIGO VESPUCCI* PUTS IN AT MARSEILLES, THE ATTENTION SHE ATTRACTS IS NO LESS THAN WHEN SHE SAILED FOR THE FIRST TIME. THE *MALTESE FALCON*, THE MOST MODERN AND MOST MAJESTIC OF TALL SHIPS, RECENTLY LAUNCHED AT LA SPEZIA, MADE THE

INTRODUCTION On the Wings of Beauty

BAY SEEM A POND AND THE GUESTS WERE BEWITCHED BY SUCH A GLORIOUS SIGHT. A GREAT SAILING SHIP RE-NEWS THE TECHNICAL AND HUMAN CHALLENGE THROWN DOWN BY THE MYSTERY OF THE SEA.

STAD AMSTERDAM, A DUTCH CLIPPER MODELED ON THE *CUTTY SARK*, WAS SAILING THE MEDITERRANEAN A SHORT WHILE AGO. IT SEEMS THAT WHEN SHE WAS PREPARING TO HOST THE SAILS WHILE LYING OFF GENOA, THIS BEAUTIFUL SHIP WAS ROLLING SO MUCH THAT ALMOST ALL THE GUESTS ON BOARD WERE VIO-LENTLY SICK. WHEN THEY RETURNED ASHORE, EVERY-ONE AGREED THE DAY HAD BEEN "HELL." WHEN I SPOKE TO SOME OF THEM BY PHONE A FEW DAYS LATER THEY

On the Wings of Beauty
Introduction

DESCRIBED THE EXPERIENCE, WITH THE NAUSEA AND GRIMNESS STILL FRESH IN THEIR MINDS. BUT WHEN ASKED "HOW WAS IT?" THEY ANSWERED "FABULOUS…" NOW THAT THE WARMING OF THE PLANET HAS BECOME THE GREAT TOPIC OF OUR TIMES, TALL SHIPS SEEM AS UP TO DATE AS EVER. THEY PLY THE OCEANS WITHOUT POLLUTING THEM, SAILING FOR DAY AFTER DAY URGED ON ONLY BY THE WIND, WHILE ALL AROUND EVERYONE RUSHES BY AT SUPERSONIC SPEEDS. THEIR SLOWNESS IS EVEN TOUCHING. ABOVE ALL, IN VIEW OF THE GENERAL DISGUST WITH MODERN DESIGN, THEY EVEN MANAGE TO BE BEAUTIFUL. FORTUNATELY FOR US, THERE WILL NEVER BE A SEA WITHOUT TALL SHIPS.

● Training aboard *Sorlandet*, in Stavanger, Norway.

648 • A golden figurehead decorates
the bow of the *Amerigo Vespucci*.

648-649 • The *Amerigo Vespucci* is
the Italian navy's training ship.

650 ● Although modern ships are entirely different from those of the past, courses on training ships are an essential part of learning naval discipline and understanding orders and terminology, in other words finding out about life at sea.

650-651 ● Once upon a time sailors were regarded as "the damned." They had a short life and no right of redress against their captains. Today, the navy is one of the last bastions of a set of essential values and an age-old tradition.

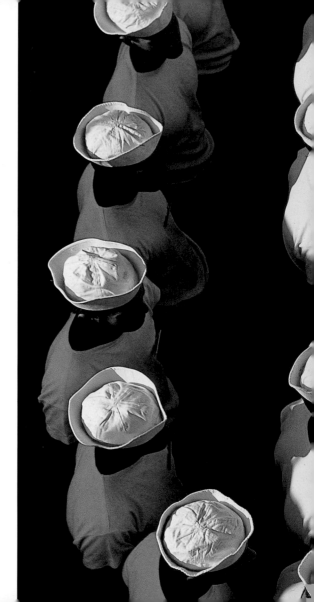

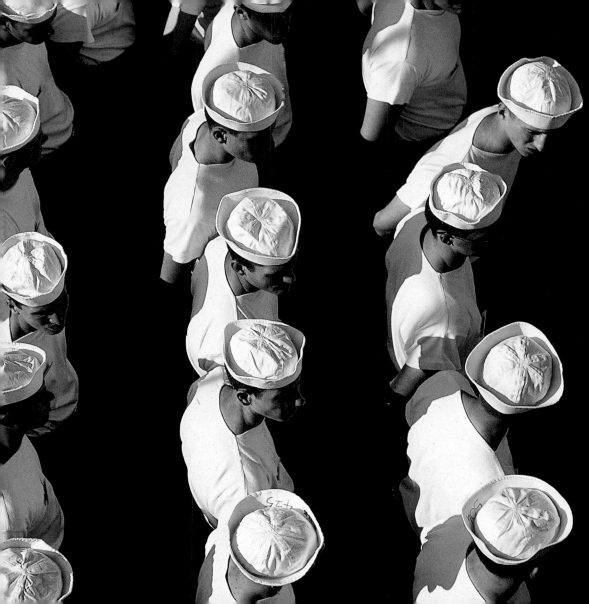

652 ● Only on a training ship (here the *Vespucci*) can one discover how important teamwork is.

652-653 ● A moment of rest aboard the *Amerigo Vespucci*.

654 • On a tall ship the size of the *Amerigo Vespucci* every detail has to be kept in ship-shape and done in Bristol fashion.

654-655 • The astonishing number of lines on the *Amerigo Vespucci* gives an idea of how complicated it is to carry out maneuvers.

656-657 • The *Amerigo Vespucci*'s steering gear combines a blend of classic and ultramodern.

657 • The steering gear and instruments on the *Vespucci*'s bridge are used when under sail.

658 ● The figurehead of HMS *Rose*.

658-659 ● HMS *Rose* is the replica of a Royal Navy frigate launched in the 18th century and employed during the American War of Independence.

660-661 ● HMS *Rose* hoists heavy canvas sails.

662 ● The figurehead of the
Royal Clipper.

662-663 ● The *Royal Clipper* has
the honour of being the largest tall
ship in the world, with five masts
and square sails. Her 42 sails are
a unique spectacle when they
are all set, as in this photograph.

664 • The *Mircea* is a barque dating from 1938, one of the so-called "Five Sisters," namely the five identical tall ships, around 269 ft (82 m) in length, built in Hamburg by the Blohm & Voss shipyards.

665 • The *Star Flyer*, the *Star Clipper*'s twin, can accommodate 170 guests, has four masts and almost 43,055 sq. ft (4000 sq. m) of sail area.

- The barque *Statsraad Lehmkuhl*, 1516 tonnes, was built in 1914 in the Johann C. Tecklenborg shipyard in Geestemünde and launched with the name *Grossherzog Friedrich August*. This ship makes an impressive sight at sea – 275.5 ft (84 m) long and 41.3 ft (12.60 m) wide.

668 • The *Simón Bolívar*, a barque built in 1978 by the Celeya shipyards in Bilbao,
is the Venezuelan navy's training ship.

669 • In spite of a gross tonnage of 1250 tons, thanks to her steel hull, the *Simón Bolívar*
is here seen heeling slightly with the wind on the beam.

670 • The hands climb to the masthead on *Pogoria*, launched in 1980.

671 • The *Pogoria* on a broad reach. This Polish brig has a length of almost 164 ft (50 m) and is used for training purposes.

The *Mir* at sunset. Built by the Danzig shipyards for the Soviet Navy in 1987, the *Mir* is a training ship.

674 • The Polish navy's training ship, the triple-masted *Dar Mdlodziezy* measures 354 ft (108 m) stem to stern and was built in Danzig in 1981.

674-675 • The *Tovarishch*, launched in 1933, cruising serenely in friendly waters. But it was not always so. Built in Germany as a training ship, she was scuppered in 1945. She was assigned to the Russians, who refloated and renamed her in 1950.

676 and 677 • The *Eagle* was launched in Hamburg on 30th June 1936 and sailed under the German flag with the name *Horst Wessel* before being awarded to the Americans after the Second World War as part of war reparations.

678-679 • The *Cuauhtémoc*, the training ship of the Mexican National Navy, bears the name of the last Aztec emperor. At 295 ft (90 m) in lenght and carrying 25,488 sq. ft (2368 sq. m) of sail, she is regarded as a symbol of Mexican sailing prowess.

680 • An Ecuadorean sailor at work on a yard on board the *Guayas*.

681 • The *Guayas* on a broad reach. She is the training ship of the Ecuadorean navy.

682 ● A sailor clews up a high sail while balancing on the lower shrouds.

682-683 ● The *Kruzenshtern* was built in 1926 by the J. G. Tecklenborg shipyard in Bremerhaven/Wesermünde, in Germany. She is 374 ft (114 m) in lenght and has a gross tonnage of 2678 tons and displacement of 5750.

684 ● Two cadets balancing and at attention on the *Libertad*.

684-685 ● The *Libertad* was built for the Argentine navy in 1956 in the Astilleros y Fabricas Navales del Estado shipyard in Rio Santiago (Buenos Aires, Argentina). Today she is a training ship.

686 • The *Danmark* with the wind abeam. The enormous size and weight of these tall ships
means they need a huge number of sails.

687 • The *Danmark*'s figurehead.

688-689 • The *Stad Amsterdam* at sea. This clipper is a replica of the *Cutty Sark* and operates as a charter ship around the world.

689 • The sails are arranged asymmetrically to increase as much as possible the *Stad Amsterdam*'s speed in light Mediterranean breezes.

690 • The *Juan Sebastián de Elcano* at dusk. Launched in 1928, she is now the training ship of the Spanish navy.

691 • The splendid bow of the *Juan Sebastián de Elcano*. The ship is almost 328 ft (100 m) in lenght and 43.14 ft (13.15 m) wide and bears the name of Magellan's famous traveling companion in the South Seas.

Thoroughly restored after the First World War, the *Cristian Radich* was relaunched in 1937, in Norway. The *Radich* is regarded as one of the best training ships still operating. Her length is 246.7 ft (75.20 m) overall.

● The *Belem* in a strong wind. The topmost sails have been clewed up and the bow
is buried in the sea as the ship plows on. Launched in France in 1896, the *Belem*
has changed hands several times: she became English in 1913 and Irish in 1921, before
flying the Italian flag until 1979, when she returned to France.

696 • Sailors on board the *Belem* prepare to climb up to work on the high sails.

696-697 • The *Belem* in a storm: the bow bursts spectacularly out of a wave.

• Launched under the name of *Don Juan de Austria* in 1953, the *Esmeralda* was given to Chile by Spain in 1954 to pay off debts. She is one of the largest tall ships in the world, measuring 370 ft (113 m) in length.

700 • Work at the masthead of the *Esmeralda*.

700-701 • The sails are dropped. Even the simplest maneuvers on a training ship like the Chilean vessel need a considerable number of sailors and great coordination.

The wind drops. The high sails can be hoisted once again. The sailors of the *Esmeralda* training ship climb up to perform the maneuver.

The *Sagres* (whose bow sails are pictured here) was built to train the Nazi Kriegsmarine. Captured by the Americans in 1945, she was passed on first to Brazil, then Portugal.

706 ● The rudder on the *Sagres* controls a huge ship: 295 ft (90 m) in lenght and displacing 1950 tons.

707 ● The *Sagres* bears away with the wind on the beam to port, making the most of her 21,528 sq. ft 2000 sq. m) of sail.

708 ● These large training ships need great courage and an exceptional sense of balance in their crews. For the naval cadets, life on board the *Sagres*, as on all other similar vessels, teaches self-control and how to overcome one's fears.

709 ● The *Sagres* in perfect trim. The cadets can enjoy a short rest.

710-711 ● The *Alexander Von Humboldt* at sea. An officer on lookout in the bow.

711 ● The barque *Alexander Von Humboldt*, built in 1906 as a three-masted brigantine, operated as a lightship in the North Sea and Baltic Sea. Today she has become a real advertising standby.

712 • The *Nippon Maru* shows off her size among small sailing boats.

713 • The *Nippon Maru* was launched in 1930. She is almost 328 ft (100 m) long and one of the most beautiful of all training ships. Seen here at speed on a broad reach and in fine trim.

714 • The *Kruzenshtern* was launched in Belgium in 1926. She was captured by the Soviets in 1946 and today is the only ship training fishing-vessel officers.

715 • The *Kruzenshtern* is 377 ft (115 m) in lenght. Here her port bow stands out next to a catamaran.

716-717 • A cadet at work on one of the *Kruzenshtern*'s 25 sails.

717 • The *Kruzenshtern* seen from the port side as she sails on a starboard tack.

718-719 • The *Gorch Fock*, a stunning barque, shows off her elegance in this aerial shot. Note the junk mainsail in the stern.

719 • The *Gorch Fock* is about 295 ft (90 m) long and is the most prestigious training ship in the German navy.

720 • The *Nippon Maru*'s sister ship, the *Kaiwo Maru II* was launched in 1989 to replace her namesake built in 1930.

720-721 • A mass of shrouds, sheets and sails covers the *Kaiwo Maru*'s deck.

722 • The "pocket ship" *Georg Stage* (177 ft/54 m in lenght) is the Danish merchant navy's training ship. She was launched in 1935.

722-723 • Young Danish cadets haul on a sheet on the *Georg Stage*.

724 • A dizzying view of the bridge of the *Star Flyer* from the masthead. This luxurious
vessel is used exclusively as a charter yacht for tourists.

725 • The *Star Flyer* sliding through the bay of Phang Nga, in Thailand, needing
only a small proportion of her 36,220 sq. ft (3365 sq. m) of sail.

726-727 • The *Star Flyer* is the *Star Clipper*'s sister ship. With her gross tonnage of 3025 tons and measuring 377 ft (115 m) in length, she is one of the largest tall ships in the world.

727 • Compared with most tall ships, the *Star Flyer* seems to be able to maneuver much more easily.

AUTHORS Biographies   INDEX

■ VALERIA MANFERTO DE FABIANIS

She is the editor of the series. Valeria Manferto De Fabianis was born in Vercelli, Italy and studied arts at the Università Cattolica del Sacro Cuore in Milan, graduating with a degree in philosophy.

She is an enthusiastic traveler and nature lover. She has collaborated on the production of television documentaries and articles for the most prestigious Italian specialty magazines and has also written many photography books.

She co-founded Edizioni White Star in 1984 with Marcello Bertinetti and is the editorial director.

■ SIMONE PEROTTI

(www.simoneperotti.it) was born in Rome in 1965 and divides his time between Milan and La Spezia. He is extremely keen on sailing in the open sea, especially during the winter, and is a qualified skipper and sailing instructor. He writes for literary and yachting magazines, including Yacht & Style, Yacht Capital, Style (Corriere della Sera), and Dove. He has published stories in printed and on-line literary journals, and has written two books, Zenzero e Nuvole and Stojan Decu, l'altro uomo, both published by Bompiani. Simone Perotti also reviews nautical books for SailBook (book section at www.ilmarinaio.com), the only on-line magazine dedicated to nautical publishing. His new novel Una Storia di mare was published by Bompiani in January 2007.

INDEX

PHOTO CREDITS

PHOTO CREDITS

● A dawn start with a following breeze.

Cover ● The American schooner *Lelantina*, sailing since the thirties,
is one of the most beautiful of John Alden's boat designs.

Back cover ● America's Cup 2007: *Alinghi*'s bow steals the show in front of Emirates New Zealand.